Alastair Sawday's

Special
places to stay

PARIS HOTELS

Edited by Ann Cooke-Yarborough

Typesetting, Conversion & Repro:	Avonset, Bath
Maps:	Springboard Design, Bristol
Printing:	Midas Book Printers, UK
Design:	Caroline King & Springboard Design, Bristol
UK Distribution:	Portfolio, Greenford, Middlesex
US Distribution:	The Globe Pequot Press, Guilford, Connecticut

Published in January 2001

Alastair Sawday Publishing Co. Ltd
The Home Farm, Barrow Gurney, Bristol BS48 3RW

The Globe Pequot Press
P. O. Box 480
Guilford, Connecticut 06437
USA

Third edition 2001

ISBN 1-901970-13-2 in the UK

ISBN 0-7627-0773-9 in the US

Printed in Slovenia

The publishers have made every effort to ensure the accuracy of the information in the book at the time of going to press. However, they cannot accept any responsibility for any loss, injury or inconvenience resulting from the use of information contained in this guide.

Alastair Sawday's

Special
places to stay

Paris Hotels

J'aime... tendrement Paris jusqu'à ses verrues et à ses taches;
...la gloire de la France et l'un des plus nobles ornements du monde.

I love Paris tenderly, even her warts and her spots;
...the glory of France and one of the world's noblest ornaments.
Michel de Montaigne (1533-1592)

Guilford
Connecticut, USA

Alastair Sawday Publishing
Bristol, UK

Contents

Contents

Contents

Contents

Acknowledgements

Ann Cooke-Yarborough has done it again! I can hardly begin to describe to you the ineffable difficulties of putting this book together. Paris hoteliers are so under siege that their instinct is to resist any intrusion by outsiders, any attempt to winkle something out of them. (We charge for entry.) Life is hard enough for them without having to think of this. Besides, the Internet is - surely - the panacea for it all. Books will soon be passés, non?

Well, Ann has trudged the streets, wearing out a good pair of shoes. She has peeked into the darkest corners of some astonishing places, ferreted out the hotels that we are all looking for. She has beguiled, cajoled, persuaded and informed - always with immense courtesy and good humour. Finally, she has been trusted by all these hotel-owners to produce this book with passion and conviction, and with a huge amount of skill. She has done so, and remains our Most Distinguished Editor.

In Memoriam: we have included a few of John Pruen's remarkable and highly personal drawings in memory of a fine gentleman and of his particular sense of humour. Sadly, he died in 1999.

Alastair Sawday

Series Editor:	Alastair Sawday
Editor:	Ann Cooke-Yarborough
Production Manager:	Julia Richardson
Managing Editor:	Annie Shillito
Accounts:	Jenny Purdy
Paris support team:	Susan Luraschi Brendan Flanagan
All things web:	Russell Wilkinson
PR/Marketing:	Jayne Warren
Title page illustrations:	Celia Witchard
Cartoons:	John Pruen
Furniture drawings:	Mathias Fournier
Symbols:	Mark Brierley

Introduction

The hotel 'scene' in Paris gets worse and worse, or better and better. It rather depends on your point of view.

If you are a shareholder of a major corporation that is doing nicely out of hotel acquisitions, then you may be content with the way things are working for you. One by one the fine old family-owned hotels of Paris - the ones that millions of us have loved for years - are being gobbled up and transformed. The exteriors are kept, but the insides are 'remodelled' in a cloud of dust. Out go the families, the staff, the furniture and the style. With them go the character and the integrity. In comes a wholly new approach to running a hotel: the 'bottom-line' is king and everything is done with an eye to cost, replaceability, standardisation. So it should be, of course, in a modern business with shareholders.

If however, you are wearing your 'human being' hat - and many of the above shareholders wear that hat quite often - then your response might be one of outrage and despair. Yet another bastion of individuality is seen to tumble. Where is the Paris you have once loved? Where are those indefinable smells, sounds and characters that have for so long made the fabric of the city? Instead we have more scaffolding, more clouds of dust and whirring of cranes, more steel and glass, crisp lines and easy predictability - the efficient workings of a system to which so many of us subscribe, when wearing another hat.

But there is a candle spluttering in the darkness! This book is that candle, for within its pages are the hundred or so places that are bravely flying the flag for the Paris we love. Their owners are hard-working, determined - even stubborn. They fight a tax system that makes it hard to employ people, and an economic system with no heart. They are fighting for the right to be authentic, so go and support them. Funnily enough, they also provide some of the best rooms, the best value, the best conversation and the most interesting experiences still to be had in Paris.

Alastair Sawday

Introduction

What has changed since 1998 in "the most beautiful city in the world"*? Riding on two booms - the economic and the crane-borne - the façade cleaners have been hard at work and the great buildings on either side of the Seine glow pale as pure new stone - almost too beautiful to be honest (*trop beau pour être honnête*), but time and pollution will soon solve that, because the air of Paris has not got perceptibly cleaner. We just have daily information about its 'quality' (the worst level is *exécrable*). So help keep pollution down, save yourself long and frustrating hunts for rare and expensive parking spaces and use the excellent public transport system - there are more bus corridors every year and metro stations are being redecorated with a fascinating variety of styles and messages (cf. Making the Most of Paris).

And the hotels of Paris? As we have already said, the scene changes all the time. I am sorry to say that Madame Bruel, a monument of the Paris hotel scene, has had enough and is selling her legendary *Hôtel Esmeralda*. With her goes an extraordinarily special place to stay, known and loved by generations of travellers from all over the world. The *Esmeralda* catered for the unwealthy who care passionately about meeting people in authentic surroundings and little about designer fabrics and the latest in bathroom fittings. She will be missed by many. Otherwise, some continue unchanged, some hand over to the next generation, some newcomers bring excitingly different attitudes to the small hotel world.

Who is in this book?

This new edition of *Paris Hotels* has been a pleasure to research. The big chains are trying to move into the small, charming hotel market but there is still a solid bunch of owners - long-standing or new to the profession, individuals, families or small partnerships - who want fiercely to remain independent and to cater for the individual traveller rather than for tour-operated groups. These are the people whom we have invited - and who have accepted - to appear in these pages.

Their average age is falling - an encouraging trend; they are enthusiastic and likeable with a sincere interest in people. Their interest in renewing the appearance of their hotels is exciting, too. Lastly, I salute the trend towards beautiful birdcages housing... beautifully-crafted fake birds.

What to expect

We hope to have explained the individuality and quirks of each hotel so that you will only choose a place that suits you. The range in these pages is broad, from our one and only *Pension de Famille*, a French institution that is definitely only for those who know and want exactly that kind of homely

* Paris City Council campaign to persuade Parisians to love their home town.

Introduction

simplicity, to two or three rather grand establishments where superior comfort comes with genuine attentiveness - at four-star prices. Obviously, the smaller the hotel, the more personal the welcome. But do read our write-ups closely for details and atmosphere.

Space

The greatest luxury in Paris is space. Even the more expensive hotel rooms are generally small but there are exceptions - we tell you about them all.

Noise

This dense, populous city is on a wonderfully human scale but it is noisy, and late-night revelry under your window or, more annoyingly, a stream of cars, can be part of the package. More and more hotels are fitting double glazing and air conditioning but if you are a fresh air fiend and can't sleep with the windows shut, bring your earplugs. Or ask for a room *sur la cour* (over the courtyard) - it won't have a stunning view but it will be quieter. Other noise, in the cheaper hotels, can be due to thin walls and televisions - or those late-night revellers on their way to bed. It's hard to know what to do about this - earplugs again, or try asking the next morning for a quieter room at the end of the corridor.

How to use this book

Rooms

Each hotel has a variety of rooms: singles, doubles, twins, so specify your requirements on booking. All bedrooms have their own bath or shower room with wc unless otherwise stated.

Family suites

Most hotels can turn two double rooms into a self-contained suite so do enquire when booking.

Disabled

In effect, any hotel with a lift has rooms accessible to people of limited mobility but some lifts start from the first floor: check when booking.

Prices

The Single & Double room price range covers the lowest price for one person to the highest for two people. Differences may be due to seasons, room size, style or comfort, so the variations within those ranges can be considerable.

Taxe de séjour

Paris City Council levies a tax per person per night in Paris hotels. It is

Introduction

currently 3 Frs for 1-star, 5 Frs for 2-star, 6 Frs for 3-star, 7 Frs for 4-star. Some hotels include it in the price, some add it on - we can't specify which so be prepared for a small extra sum per day on the bill.

Credit Cards

Only the Pension des Marronniers does not take credit cards. MasterCard and Visa are universally accepted; American Express sometimes; Diners Card hardly ever.

Breakfast

Unless we say otherwise, it will be basic Continental: coffee, tea or chocolate with baguette, butter and jam plus a possible croissant and orange juice. Continental Plus means this with, perhaps, cereals, yoghurt and/or fruit. Buffet can be a help-yourself Continental Plus or a fabulous spread that virtually provides your daily intake of calories in one sitting. Breakfast in bed will almost always be Continental. To make the most of every square centimetre, Paris hotel breakfast rooms are often in their stone vaulted cellars. Magnificent examples of a well-tried building principle, they are, of course, 'authentic', 'original', 'fascinating', but they can be rather stuffy and 'close'.

Telephones

With few exceptions, all rooms have telephones; some can even supply a private line with your own number. Remember, however, to use hotel telephones only in extremis or if you are rich. The bills rarely fail to raise eyebrows, and temperatures.

Our telephone numbers give the standard ten-digit French number, e.g. (0)1 23 45 67 89.

- to dial from any telephone **inside** France, dial all ten digits, including the bracketted zero, e.g. 01 23 45 67 89;

- to dial from **outside** France, use your international access code then the country code for France - 33 - and the last 9 digits of the number you want, e.g. 00 33 1 23 45 67 89;

- numbers beginning (0)6 are mobile phone numbers and will cost you accordingly;

- to telephone from France -
  - to Great Britain, dial 00 44 and your correspondent's number without its initial zero,
  - to the USA, dial 00 1 and your correspondent's number without its initial zero.

Introduction

Pillows and tea

If there is something you need and can't see, ask for it. The hotel may or may not be able to provide but you can only find out by asking. If you don't like the bolster they have put on the bed, look in the cupboard for a pillow. If it's not there, ask. If you're particular about your tea, take your favourite tea-bags with you - French tea is often fairly standard.

Problems

If you have a problem, please first bring it up with the hotel owner or manager: they are the obvious people to ask for immediate action. Do remember that you are paying to be looked after and if your hot water isn't hot or your bed isn't made by 5pm, well... it should be! Also, the manager's job is to keep you as happy as possible - he wants you to come back - but he can't solve a problem he doesn't know about. So do give them a chance to sort it out. However, if you try and don't succeed, or if you experience downright rudeness, then we need to know. Please write to us in such a case.

Parking

We tell you which hotels have their own car-parking arrangements, but do not take these for granted: space must be booked at the same time as the room. The charge should be something between 80 Frs and 150 Frs per day, though I have heard of one garage that charges 250 Frs per day.

Tipping

French services - restaurants, cafés, hotels - must charge including TVA (French sales tax) so one should only tip for exceptional service or kindness.

Two Parisian anecdotes, October 2000

City of arrogant individuals or community-minded human beings?

1. In Friday evening rush hour traffic on Rue de Rivoli, the bus corridor is blocked by a parked car so the No 67 starts pulling out, to the fury of a man driving a big Mercedes. His unmoving insistence on his right to that spot in the jam ("buses should keep to their corridors") costs him a wing mirror and an apoplectic fit: he shouts, screams, insults the young bus driver, whose passengers are up in arms in his defence. At last, Monsieur Mercedes explodes with "You stupid little 6000-franc-a-month employee - I know people who will make sure you lose your stupid little job for this!"

Thereupon, the passengers - all, of course, employees not possessed of big cars - pour into the road to give Monsieur M a piece of their collective mind; prudently, he retreats back into his steel castle; the passengers give

Introduction

their names and addresses to 'their' driver, "in case you need us to witness for you"; and the No 67 pursues its normal slow Friday evening course.(With thanks to Pierre Georges of *Le Monde*.)

2. 8.45am on a weekday morning. The soft-voiced woman on the telephone asks me "do I own a car with such-and-such a number plate?". Yes, I do. "Well, the entrance you're blocking is needed so you'd better move your car". Who could know my name and telephone number with just my car registration number? Only the police... Instead of issuing a fine or calling in the towing company, the little local Commissariat had looked into the central police file and taken the trouble to ring me up. I am still moved by the thought of such kindness from official quarters, if a little disquieted by the efficiency of the state's information system.

Examples of genuine solidarity among ordinary people are still to be found in the fast and furious stampede towards MORE.

Environment

We seek to reduce our impact on the environment where possible by:

- Planting trees to compensate for our carbon emissions (as calculated by Edinburgh University); we are officially a carbon-neutral publishing company.

- Re-using paper, recycling stationery, tins, bottles, etc.

- Encouraging staff use of bicycles (they're given free) and encouraging car-sharing.

- Celebrating the use of organic, home and locally-produced food.

- Publishing books that support, in however minor a way, small-scale businesses.

Subscriptions

Hotels pay to appear in this guide; their fee goes towards the high production costs of an all-colour book. We really do only include places and owners that we find special. It is not possible for anyone to buy their way in.

Special Places to Stay on the Internet: www.sawdays.co.uk

By the time you read this we will have roughly a thousand entries on the online database which is our web site. These are from the various titles in the *Special Places to Stay* series, so if you like the places in this book, why not browse some more?

Introduction

We flatter ourselves that the 8,000 visitors a month who come to the site have good reason to, and we think you should join them! It gives access to hundreds of places to stay across Europe and you can buy all our books direct through our window on the world wide web.

Disclaimer

We make no claims to pure objectivity in judging our *Special Places to Stay*. They are here because we like them. Our opinions and tastes are ours alone and this book is a statement of them; we hope you will share them.

We have done our utmost to get our facts right but apologise for any mistakes that may have crept in. Sometimes, too, prices shift, usually upwards and 'things' change. We should be grateful to be told of any errors and changes.

Finally

Do let us know how you got on in these hotels - we value your feedback and recommendations enormously. There is a report form at the back of the book or email **parishotels@sawdays.co.uk**.

And please tell the management that you found their hotel in this book.

Happy travelling!

18

General Map with Arrondissements

Detailed maps are shown on the following pages.

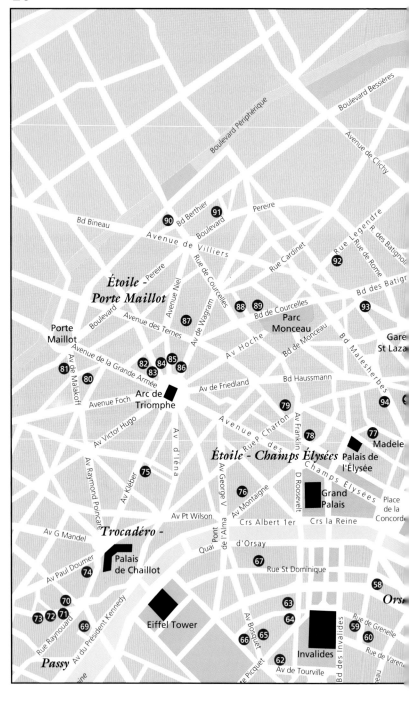

Scale

1 mi

1 km

Map 1

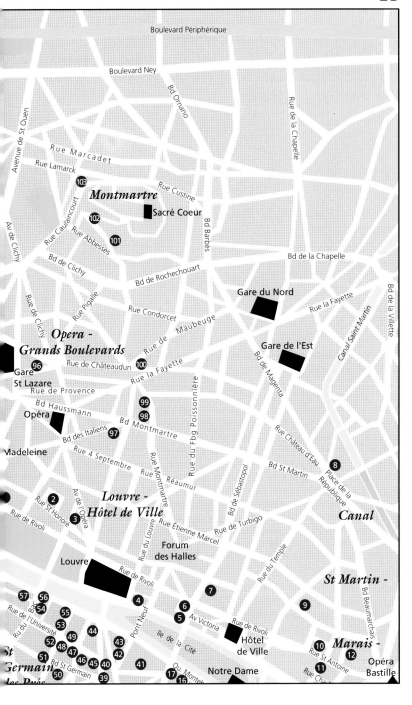

Map 2

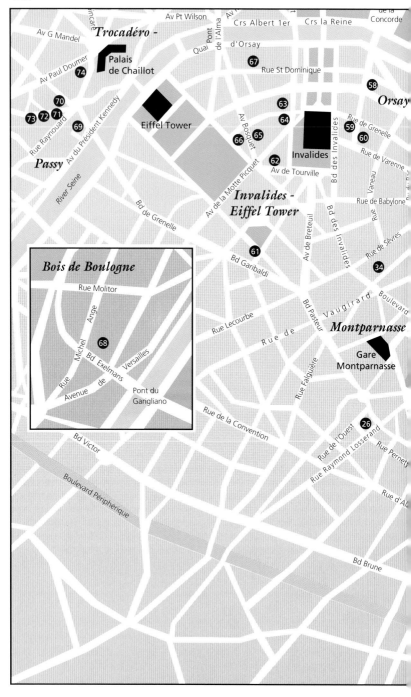

Trocadéro -

Av Pt Wilson

Av G Mandel

Crs Albert 1er

Crs la Reine

de la Concorde

Quai Pont de l'Alma

d'Orsay

Palais de Chaillot

Av Paul Doumer

74

Rue St Dominique

67

58

Orsay

70

73 **72** **71**

69

Eiffel Tower

63

64

Rue de Grenelle

59

60

66 **65**

62

Invalides

Rue de Varenne

Passy

Rue Raynouard

Av du Président Kennedy

River Seine

Av Bosquet

Av de Tourville

Rue de Babylone

Rue Vaneau

Bd de Grenelle

Invalides - Eiffel Tower

Av de la Motte Picquet

Av de Breteuil

Bd des Invalides

Rue de Sèvres

34

Bois de Boulogne

61

Bd Garibaldi

Rue Molitor

Rue Michel Ange

Bd Exelmans

Avenue de Versailles

68

Rue Lecourbe

Rue Pasteur

Vaugirard Boulevard

Montparnasse

Rue de

Gare Montparnasse

Pont du Garigliano

Rue Falguière

Bd Victor

Rue de la Convention

Rue de l'Ouest

Rue Raymond Losserand

Rue Pernety

26

Rue d'Al

Boulevard Périphérique

Bd Brune

Scale   1 mil

1 km

Map 3

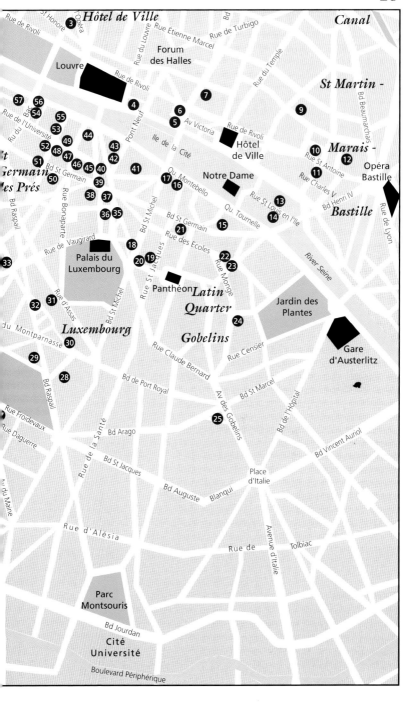

Map 4

Plan of Paris Metro System

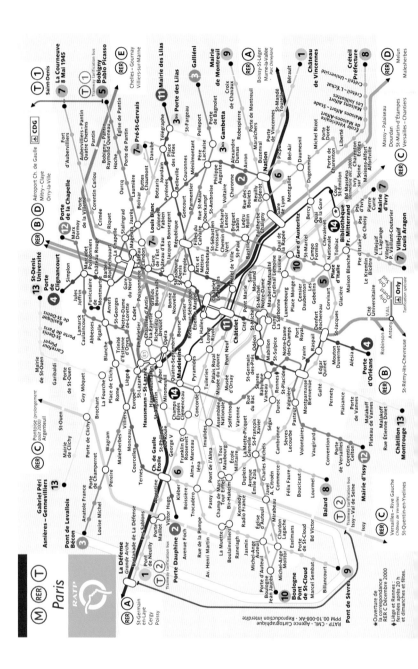

Rue de Rivoli & Tuileries Gardens
•
Palais Royal
•
Forum des Halles
•
St Eustache
•
Pompidou Centre
•
St Germain l'Auxerrois

Louvre – Hôtel de Ville

 small

 som

Hôtel Brighton

218 rue de Rivoli
75001 Paris

Tel: (0)1 47 03 61 61
Fax: (0)1 42 60 41 78
E-mail: hotel.brighton@wanadoo.fr
Web: www.esprit-de-france.com

Jean-Louis Lebouc

Standing proud over the arches of the Rue de Rivoli, looking straight through gold-tipped railings to the French formality of the Tuileries gardens, the Brighton is true turn-of-the-century grand: mosaic floor, fluted columns, glittering chandeliers in a dining room that is soberly ivory and grey, full of arcaded light, soft-ginger monogrammed Philippe Starck chairs and no knick-knacks. Deep renovation is still in progress but, although the refurbished rooms are very fine, any room at the front is worth having for the experience of belonging to that view, and the higher the better (NB 1st-floor rooms are under the arcades). Most are a decent size; renovated rooms are really big, finely-corniced, cool-walled and warm-clothed, some have an original fireplace or a vast mirrored armoire and all have superb bathrooms. Older rooms have... older bathrooms (still perfectly adequate); some are prettily redecorated with sponged walls and plain carpets; elsewhere, the original décor is a reminder of the 1970s, often characterful, sometimes a little weary. But improvements come apace. And the young manager is gentle and attentive. *Ask reception about modem adapters.*

Rooms: 65.
Price: Singles, doubles, junior suites
685-1200 Frs (€104.43-182.94).
Breakfast: 45 Frs.
Meals: On request 100-200 Frs.
Metro: Tuileries.
RER: Châtelet-Les Halles.
Bus routes: 72
Car park: Place Vendôme.

This hotel was named in the 1890s in celebration of the Entente Cordiale between staid Victorian England and giddy *Belle-Époque* France — funny thing, diplomacy.

Entry No: 1   Map No: 2

Hôtel des Tuileries
10 rue Saint-Hyacinthe
75001 Paris

Tel: (0)1 42 61 04 17
Fax: (0)1 49 27 91 56
E-mail: htuileri@aol.com
Web: members.aol.com/htuileri

Jean-Jacques Vidal

The charming Tuileries feels rather like a family house: the owners have been here for several generations. The many oriental rugs — most of them on walls — sit well in the quiet old *Relais Silence* building as its delicate listed façade moves skywards to the rhythm of balconies, arches and mouldings. Great doors give onto a white hall with rugs, mirrors, pictures old and new, leading to the elegant little *salons*. A pretty lightwell illuminates this space and the basement breakfast room while a curving staircase leads upwards. The oriental element is general but never excessive: one room is like a soft Persian tent, another has a clever draping of yellow cloth over a white bed, there are Chinese-vase table lamps, paisley fabrics. Colours are skilfull — a white room has dark blue carpet, pale blue damask curtains and bedcover, a richly-coloured rug behind the delightful cane bedhead. Lighting is good, there are pretty antiques, country pieces, modern units, good marble bathrooms. Smaller rooms can feel cramped, the higher prices are for the excellent de luxe rooms. *Family apartments possible.*

Rooms: 26.
Price: Singles & doubles 790-1400 Frs (€120.43-213.43).
Breakfast: Buffet 70 Frs.
Meals: On request.
Metro: Tuileries, Pyramides.
RER: Opéra-Auber.
Bus routes: 72
Car park: Marché St Honoré.

St Hyacinth was made a Dominican by St Dominic himself, 8 centuries ago. He then dashed all over Eastern Europe, converting the tribes and earning the title of *Apostle of the North.*

Map No: 2   **Entry No: 2**

Hôtel Londres-Saint Honoré

13 rue Saint Roch
75001 Paris

Tel: (0)1 42 60 15 62
Fax: (0)1 42 60 16 00
E-mail:
hotel.londres.st.honore@gofornet.com

Monsieur & Madame
Berthoud

In the middle of the Louvre-Opera-Concorde triangle, there is something really appealing about the Berthouds' hotel. Lots of red gives it a rich feel, as does Madame's warm voice that welcomes you: this is a new career for her and she is thoroughly enjoying it. If you ask what that intriguing antique was designed for, she doesn't know either but is delighted to share the joke. Quantities of timbers speak of age and venerability: she once found an American guest climbing the lovely staircase on all fours, reverently stroking each timber. The old building seems to turn several corners: rooms are all shapes and sizes, mostly larger than the two-star average, and the red, white and blue colour scheme is used to great effect. It is uncluttered, unfrilled and extremely pleasant with decent tiled bathrooms and pretty lights. The first-floor sitting and breakfast rooms, also easy, unaffected and light, are hung with an artist friend's most decorative paintings. Their second hotel, the plainer Saint Roch just up the road, a kind of 22-room 'annexe', is being done up in the same style as the Saint Honoré. *Internet access in salon. Lift from 1st floor reception level.*

Rooms: 29, including 1 suite for 5/6.
Price: Singles & doubles 400-600 Frs (€60.98-91.47), suite 1225 Frs.
Breakfast: 40 Frs.
Meals: No.
Metro: Tuileries, Pyramides.
RER: Châtelet-Les Halles.
Bus routes: 21 27 29 68 95
Car park: Pyramides.

The tiny antique shop clinging to the church opposite may indeed have been founded in 1638 but until recently it also announced *Coiffeur de Napoléon*. He was a small man...

Entry No: 3   Map No: 2

Le Relais du Louvre

19 rue des Prêtres St Germain l'Auxerrois
75001 Paris

Tel: (0)1 40 41 96 42
Fax: (0)1 40 41 96 44
E-mail: au-relais-du-louvre@dial.oleane.com

Sophie Aulnette

Look down the throats of gargoyles. Soak up the history: the Revolutionaries printed their newsletter in the cellar; it inspired Puccini's Café Momus in *Bohême*; it still rings with the famous carillon next door... and it's an utterly delightful place, with charming young managers who greet you from their low antique desk. Antiques and oriental rugs complement the modernity of firm beds and perfect bathrooms. Front rooms look onto the church's Gothic windows and flying buttresses and down to the austerely neo-Classical Louvre; others give onto a light-filled patio. Top-floor junior suites have twin beds and a non-convertible sofa (no cluttering up), pastel walls, exuberant upholstery and heaps of light from mansard windows. The apartment (illustrated) is big and beautiful with fireplace, books, music, old engravings and a superb veranda kitchen. Other, smaller rooms are luminous, fresh and restful — yellow, a favourite colour, brings sunny moods into small spaces. You feel softly secluded and coddled everywhere. The sense of service is tremendous and, as there is no breakfast room, breakfast comes to you. *On each floor, two rooms can make a family suite.*

Rooms: 21, including 2 junior suites & 1 apartment.
Price: Singles & doubles 650-1050 Frs (€99.09-160.07); suites 1300-1500 Frs; apartment 2500 Frs.
Breakfast: 60 Frs (served in bedroom).
Meals: On request 50-150 Frs.
Metro: Louvre-Rivoli, Pont Neuf.
RER: Châtelet-Les Halles.
Bus routes: 68 69 72
Car park: Card at hotel.

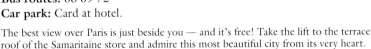

The best view over Paris is just beside you — and it's free! Take the lift to the terrace roof of the Samaritaine store and admire this most beautiful city from its very heart.

Map No: 2 & 4

Entry No: 4

Grand Hôtel de Champagne

13 rue des Orfèvres
75001 Paris

Tel: (0)1 42 36 60 00
Fax: (0)1 45 08 43 33

Madame Lauferon &
Monsieur Herbon

 50 Frs △ ▽

Old, alive with history and timbers, the Champagne was built in 1562 (spot the date on the wooden pillar by reception) on a street corner that was first recorded in the 13th century. Over the ages, it has been a monastery, a school and an inn: rooms were never big, corridors twisted and turned round the corner and the vast expanse of the panelled lobby does not prepare you for the more medieval proportions upstairs. The very smart Louis XIII dining room is big too, in its crimson and gold regalia. This is where you can indulge in a remarkably full and varied breakfast buffet. Bedrooms are sweetly, cosily cottagey, with more timbers and beams, cords and canopy effects, spriggy or stripey wallpapers, the odd little antique and glances at the great periods of French style — Louis XIII, XV and XVI. There are nooks, corners and crannies, as dictated by the ancient layout, and the smart suites occupy two or three old rooms each. Bathrooms are imaginatively pretty. It is altogether enfolding and peaceful. Staff and manager are relaxed and smiling — he clearly likes his job and enjoys making clients as comfortable as possible. *Two floors are non-smoking.*

Rooms: 43, including 3 suites.
Price: Singles & doubles 715-960 Frs
(€109-146.35); suites 1300-1900 Frs.
Breakfast: Full buffet 70 Frs.
Meals: No.
Metro: Châtelet, Pont Neuf.
RER: Châtelet-Les Halles.
Bus routes: 21 38 58 67 69 74 76 81 85
Car park: Belle Jardinière.

For two centuries (16th-18th), the whole neighbourhood was occupied by master craftsmen and their brotherhoods : goldsmiths, silversmiths, tailors and cobblers.

Entry No: 5

Map No: 2 & 4

Hôtel Britannique

20 avenue Victoria
75001 Paris

Tel: (0)1 42 33 74 59
Fax: (0)1 42 33 82 65
E-mail: mailbox@hotel-britannique.fr
Web: www.hotel-britannique.fr

J-F Danjou

On a quietish street by the Châtelet and originally run by the (*Britannique*) Baxters, this comfortable hotel is owned by an ex-naval man with a passion for Turner: the great painter's *Jessica* greets you in the lobby, copies of his atmospheric scenes adorn corridors and bedroom walls, the *Fighting Téméraire* dominates the superbly refurbished *salon*, alongside a model galleon, an HMV gramophone horn and some fine books. There is a lush feel to the hallways but do try the staircase: elegantly pink and grey, it has handsome old fitted oak chests on each landing. The average-to-small rooms are decorated with custom-designed elements, pastel walls, heavy green-leaf/red-grape fabrics, boxes of pot-pourri for extra florality and perfectly adequate bathrooms. The top floors have views over roofs and treetops. On the avenue below, plants, furniture and birds are still sold — it's fun in the daytime. The breakfast room has been extended and prettily refurnished in blue and yellow with a long marble buffet table in a rustic alcove. It is all simply comfortable with no ancient flourishes and a generally friendly reception from staff in stripey waistcoats! *Internet access in half the rooms.*

Rooms: 40.
Price: Singles & doubles 780-1080 Frs (€118.91-164.64).
Breakfast: Buffet 67 Frs.
Meals: No.
Metro: Châtelet.
RER: Châtelet-Les Halles.
Bus routes: 21 38 58 67 69 74 76 81 85
Car park: Hôtel de Ville.

During the 1st World War, the hotel was offered to American and English Quaker volunteers tending civilian victims — a service rendered by the Quakers in wars the world over.

Map No: 2 & 4   Entry No: 6

Hôtel Saint Merry

78 rue de la Verrerie
75004 Paris

Tel: (0)1 42 78 14 15
Fax: (0)1 40 29 06 82
Web: www.france-hotel.com

Monsieur Pierre Juin

Lovers of the really old and the utterly unusual, come hither! The new owner of the St Merry simply fell in love with it too and it's so small that personal attention is guaranteed. The hotel snuggles against the late-Gothic church of St Merry: in the suite, the clock tower cornice thrusts its way into the *salon*; elsewhere flying buttresses provide the most original of bed canopies. From *brocante* and flea market came the wherewithal to make the old house worthy of its origins, neo-Gothic pieces were reworked to create this astounding environment. In reception: high-backed chairs, an elaborate pew, linen-fold panels, telephone in a confessional. Décor is sober to set off the festival of carving: original beams and stones, plain velvet or 'medieval-stripe' fabrics, great cast-iron light fittings — and surprisingly colourful bathrooms. The big rooms are almost majestic, the cheaper ones smaller and more basic; the suite with private stairs, big timbered *salon* (illustrated: Paris's only Gothic *salon?*), cosy bedroom and curious low-beamed bathroom, is a masterpiece of style and adaptation. *Difficult motor access in this pedestrian street and no lift in hotel.*

Rooms: 12.
Price: Singles & doubles 850-1200 Frs (€129.58-182.94); suite 1800-2200 Frs.
Breakfast: 60 Frs (served in bedroom).
Meals: No.
Metro: Hôtel de Ville, Châtelet.
RER: Châtelet-Les Halles.
Bus routes: 38 47 75
Car park: St Martin.

The street has been called *de la Verrerie* since 1187! The painters on glass — enamellers, glass-blowers, rosary and necklace-makers — lived and worked here for centuries.

Entry No: 7   Map No: 2 & 4

Canal St Martin
•
Place de la Republique
•
Opéra & Place de la Bastille
•
Place des Vosges
•
Picasso Museum
•
Carnavalet Museum
•
Hôtel de Sens

Canal St Martin –
Marais – Bastille

 50 F

Hôtel Gilden Magenta

35 rue Yves Toudic
75010 Paris

Tel: (0)1 42 40 17 72
Fax: (0)1 42 02 59 66
E-mail: hotel.gilden.magenta@multi-micro.com
Web: www.multi-micro.com/hotel.gilden.magent

Gilbert Pouleur

Light and air fill the lobby of this modest hotel on a little street between the tranquil waters of the Canal St Martin and the mad dash of the Place de la République. In its corner of genuine people's Paris, it has always been an hotel, one of a row of harmonious and unpretentious 1890s buildings, an old bakery on the corner. There are also one or two trendy cafés in the area now. The big hall is a real surprise, a mixture of solid angles and pure theatrical kitsch, a legacy that suits the new owners very well. They are relaxed and easy yet attentive to detail — you will be well looked after. Beyond the pretty breakfast room, the flowered and creepered patio is a delight, just the place for summer mornings beneath the giant sun-yellow parasols. The garden building has rooms that all look onto the patio. Bedrooms are impeccable but have rather less character than the ground floor: fitted laminated furniture units, carpet or cork floor tiles, plain simple décor and shower rooms, one room for four has a bit of timber framing in the middle! From some rooms at the front you can see straight down the street to the barges and boats cruising on top of the canal. A super atmosphere and excellent value.

Rooms: 32.
Price: Singles, doubles, triples 340-550 Frs (€51.83-83.85).
Breakfast: Buffet 40 Frs, 20 Frs for under 12s.
Meals: No; microwave available.
Metro: République, Jacques Bonsergent. **RER:** Gare du Nord.
Bus routes: 54 56 75
Car park: Bd Magenta (consult hotel).

The Gilden's emblem is that atmospheric footbridge where Arletty, Jouvet & Co. hang out, smoke, kiss, fight,... in Marcel Carné's iconic 1938 film *Hôtel du Nord*.

Entry No: 8   Map No: 2

Hôtel de la Bretonnerie

22 rue Sainte Croix de la Bretonnerie
75004 Paris

Tel: (0)1 48 87 77 63
Fax: (0)1 42 77 26 78
E-mail: hotel@bretonnerie.com
Web: www.bretonnerie.com

Valérie Sagot

Closed in August. The Sagots uncovered the 17th-century timber frame and created a warm, welcoming raspberry and moss nest downstairs and a great sense of enduring taste in the bedrooms. There is space and shape and the wrought-iron, wooden-railed staircase is an elegant reminder of that Parisian talent for grandeur on a human scale. The breakfast room, in a lovely bare-stone vaulted cellar, has embroidered mats and subdued lighting that adds to the Jacobean hideaway feel (there's a second vault below). Bedrooms, reached along twisty split-level corridors, past lacy corners, are all different: rich colours, old pieces and occasionally giant timbers. Some have thick wall fabric and a superior country atmosphere. One large two-windowed corner room has yellow Jouy-style 'brocade' walls, a rich brown carpet, elegant square yellow quilts across pure white bedcovers (an idea used with style throughout) and a big marble bathroom with matching wall cloth. One fine suite drips pink chintz, old furniture and... space. Bathrooms are good, some are big, and renovation continues. Last but first, the staff are really delightful and clearly love their jobs.

Rooms: 29, including 7 suites.
Price: Singles & doubles 680-870 Frs (€103.67-132.63); suites 1100 Frs.
Breakfast: Continental plus 60 Frs.
Meals: No.
Metro: Hôtel de Ville.
RER: Châtelet-Les Halles.
Bus routes: 47 72 74 75
Car park: Baudoyer.

The original *marais* (marshland), fashionable in the 17th and 18th centuries, whence all those mansions, mercifully escaped Haussmann's clean sweep in the 1860s.

Map No: 2 & 4   **Entry No:** 9

Hôtel Saint Paul le Marais

8 rue de Sévigné
75004 Paris

Tel: (0)1 48 04 97 27
Fax: (0)1 48 87 37 04
E-mail: stpaulmarais@hotellerie.net
Web: www.hotel-paris-marais.com

Michèle Leguide

In amongst the old old buildings, the cafés, boutiques and mansions of the *Marais*, this hotel, built as a convent in the 17th century, still shows a few of its original bones: timbers and pillars. The recently-renovated big red and gold lobby, with its smart brocade chairs, inviting little bar and bunched curtains, is lit from the street and from a little patio where tables can be set in summer. There is a comforting sense of welcome here, with several members of the family involved, and a massage and beauty parlour in the basement! The stone-vaulted breakfast room is down there too, for a generous and varied buffet that is worth getting up for. Bedrooms seem to be all shapes, sizes and quirks: a little child's sleeping platform with a tiny washbasin in a miniature cupboard, a muslin-canopied bed, a big bathroom with jacuzzi, another platform with a desk tucked right under a steeply-sloping ceiling, a sunny little single like a pale blue nursery. It is old-fashioned (in keeping with the building), sometimes a bit standard in its furniture, fairly floral, endearing and very friendly. Each room is soundproofed and has a kettle kit while Madame Leguide is ever willing to help and advise.

Rooms: 27.
Price: Singles & doubles 590-1140 Frs (€89.94-173.79).
Breakfast: Buffet 60 Frs.
Meals: No.
Metro: St Paul.
RER: Châtelet-Les Halles.
Bus routes: 69 76 96
Car park: Baudoyer.

Opposite, an imposing stone portal leads to Bouthillier de Chavigny's mansion — high, gracious windows and a dozen bright red chargers in the stableyard: surely the only listed fire station for miles?

Entry No: 10   Map No: 2 & 4

 small

Hôtel du 7è Art

20 rue Saint Paul
75004 Paris

Tel: (0)1 44 54 85 00
Fax: (0)1 42 77 69 10
E-mail: hotel7art@wanadoo.fr

Michel

Behind its remarkable black and white frontage, this place is as light-hearted and eternally youthful as the stars of an old American film. Besides a delightful little hotel, there is a lively bar where log fires burn in winter, warming snacks are served and you can even buy mementos of the great names of film. The people are young and charming too (those film star models), there's a laundry room in the basement and... a trio of fitness machines — to maintain your Hollywood muscles in decadent Paris. The black and white theme is pursued throughout — viz. that checked floor in the dining room — and a multitude of old film posters illuminate the walls. Up the black-carpeted stairs (*cinéma oblige*), the bedrooms are softly, unaggressively decorated — some hessian walls, some painted pine slatting, gentle brown carpets, multi-pastel piqué bedcovers and white and black bathrooms, with the odd star-studded shower curtain. Some are pretty small, some have modem sockets, all have a built-in desk top and a safe, the atmosphere is peaceful (the bar closes at midnight). And the oldest residential part of Paris is all around you. A very special place.

Rooms: 23.
Price: Singles & doubles 430-690 Frs (€65.55-105.19).
Breakfast: Continental plus 45 Frs (not served in rooms).
Meals: Bar snacks 30-100 Frs.
Metro: St Paul, Pont Marie.
RER: Châtelet-Les Halles.
Bus routes: 69 96
Car park: Pont Marie.

Just over the road, do visit the *Village St Paul*, a series of old, twisty courtyards full of antique shops and art galleries; and beyond, the remains of the 12th-century city ramparts.

Map No: 4 **Entry No:** 11

Hôtel de la Place des Vosges

12 rue de Birague   **Tel:** (0)1 42 72 60 46
75004 Paris   **Fax:** (0)1 42 72 02 64
                                  E-mail: hotel.place.des.vosges@gofornet.

Renata Sibiga

Resting on a vast beam that was already 800 years old when it was felled in the 1600s, this unpretentious hotel, one of the smallest in Paris, has kept its original muleteer's house layout: the old-furnished, comfy ground floor, so hushed after the traffic down on Rue St Antoine, was where the mule master stabled his animals; above was the hay loft, then his living quarters, and right at the top his stable boys' garrets. An air of relaxed hard work has been handed down the centuries and the new management has time to chat with visitors and advise on what to do; indeed, service and flexibility are their priorities. Expect less space above the ground floor. The tiny staircase and limited storage preclude large bags (the lift goes from 1st to 4th floors; luggage carried by staff). Rooms are being done up, bedding is new, but the décor is still simple pink and beige with tiny but perfectly adequate shower and bathrooms. An ideal family hideaway, the top floor has a view of the Bastille column from its attic windows. If you travel light, this is a wonderful part of Paris to be in, rich in history and alive with 1990s Parisians. *Cancellation policy is 72 hours notice, in writing only.*

Rooms: 16.
Price: Singles & doubles 495-900 Frs (€75.46-137.20).
Breakfast: 40 Frs.
Meals: No.
Metro: Bastille, St Paul, Sully Morland.
RER: Châtelet-Les Halles, Gare de Lyon.
Bus routes: 20 29 69 76 86 87 96
Car park: 16 rue St Antoine.

A many-titled gent: Biragues came from Italy to France in 1530 to become President of Parliament, Minister of Justice, Chancellor... Cardinal and Commander of the Holy Spirit.

Entry No: 12   Map No: 4

Hôtel du Jeu de Paume

54 rue Saint-Louis-en-l'Ile
75004 Paris

Tel: (0)1 43 26 14 18
Fax: (0)1 40 46 02 76
Web: www.hoteldujeudepaume.com

Elyane Prache &
Nathalie Heckel

 50 Frs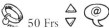

Astounding overhead: three storeys soar to the roof timbers of a 17th-century 'tennis' court. Exceptional below: genuine care from mother and daughter: fresh flowers, time for a lone guest's tales of His Day in Paris, super staff. You find a Provençal style, oodles of atmosphere, smallish rooms all giving onto inner courtyards, all different, all quiet, with careful pastelly décor, good bathrooms, old beams, tiles, stones. Duplexes have tiny staircases but more storage than others; top-floor corner rooms show the building's beautiful beamy skeleton; the fine new duplexes, one with terrace, are a delight. We love it hugely. Love it for its sense of history, eccentricities, aesthetic ironies, secluded peace and feel of home; and for its unconventional attitudes and relaxed, yet thoroughly efficient staff, so what matter that storage is limited? The sitting area is a drawing room: *objets* and deep leather sofas round a carved fireplace; breakfast is under the magnificent timbers by the surrealistic columns and glass lift; work-out is in vaulted cellars (fitness bikes, sauna, a brand new billiards table). "What really makes it different is the exceptionally polite, friendly staff": a reader.

Rooms: 30, including 2 suites.
Price: Singles & doubles 970-1660 Frs (€147.88-253.07); suites 2500-2750 Frs.
Breakfast: 80 Frs.
Meals: On request 100-350 Frs.
Metro: Pont Marie, Cité, St Paul.
RER: St Michel-Notre Dame.
Bus routes: 67
Car park: Pont Marie.

The *jeu de paume*, the Italian ancestor of tennis, was all the rage in 1634. King Louis XIII allowed developers onto the island on condition that a palm game court was built. *Plus ça change...*

Map No: 4   **Entry No:** 13

Dortoir du Pont's

13 Quai des Braves
75000 Paris

Tel: (0)1 99 99 99 99
Fax: (0)1 99 99 99 99
E-mail: dosser@clocheville.paris
Web: www.clocheville-dosser.paris

Perceval du Pont

in red bandanas

natural

Who wasn't brought up on the magic and romance of "Under the Bridges of Paris with You"? Here's the opportunity to make a dream come true. In a vastly privileged position down by the riverside, where beautiful sculptures (illustrated) take on the cloak of timelessness and the imperial gold rises to the skies of the City of Light, Perceval du Pont runs a hostelry of natural generosity for the small-pursed and light-fingered tribe. Perceval is especially proud of his collection of high-quality mattresses: passing a small hotel on his rounds one day, spotting all their good-as-new bedding on the pavement – being replaced in its prime – he seized the initiative and helped the owner give it a good home. (Since then, seizures of many sorts have been commonplace in this open-air retreat.) As he couldn't get the driver to deliver to Quai des Braves, he offered that day's clients their *gros rouge* aperitif if they collected their own beds – and all went swimmingly. His is as companionable an establishment as you could hope to find: don't come for privacy, but more for the communion with pedestrians from all walks of life, maybe even some itinerant musicians: surely better than hotel muzak.

Rooms: 1 highly adaptable space; DIY partitioning.
Price: *Paiement en liquide*: 5 litres per person per night (€ Never!).
Breakfast: Whatever you can lift.
Meals: Liquid – red or white; scrounge-your-own LVs.
Metro: Quai des Braves.
Bus routes: Shanks's pony.
Car park: Alongside.

This fine, low-slung bridge was built soon after the Eiffel Tower as another sculpted and gilded expression of France's power and glory at the turn of the century.

Entry No: 14   Map No: 4

Latin Quarter – Gobelins

Hôtel de Notre Dame

19 rue Maître Albert
75005 Paris

Tel: (0)1 43 26 79 00
Fax: (0)1 46 33 50 11

Monsieur Fouhety

A stone's throw from Notre Dame but hidden from the tourist tides in a very select little area of unusual shops and smart residences, this fine old frontage opens onto a large lobby adorned with a magnificent tapestry, bits of antiquity and deep armchairs. Openness reigns — these people genuinely like people and greet you with smiles and humour. If the age of the building (1600s) is evident in its convoluted corridors, contemporary style dictates their smart black dados with tan or sea-green uppers. Bedrooms also mix old and new. There are beams and exposed stones, some of them enormous, and Cathedral views from the higher floors, though windows are smaller up here. Most rooms have a large curvy shelf over the door that carries the discreet spotlights; custom-made desk units use the same curvy idea: a nice design, as is the new padded upholstery in warm, colourful, contemporary mixes of yellow, red and blue. The translucent Japanese screen doors to bathrooms are an excellent idea for small layouts; not all baths are full size. The black eunuch officially portrayed as Marie-Antoinette's feathered fan bearer lived here...

Rooms: 34.
Price: Singles & doubles 810-880 Frs
(€123.48-134.16).
Breakfast: 40 Frs.
Meals: No.
Metro: Maubert Mutualité.
RER: St Michel-Notre Dame.
Bus routes: 47 63 86 87
Car park: Lagrange.

Master Albert (Magister Albertus, contracted to Maubert) was a preacher, teacher, philosopher and alchemist of persuasive power. He also built a walking talking automaton — in 1254!

Entry No: 15

Map No: 4

Les Rives de Notre Dame

15 quai Saint Michel
75005 Paris

Tel: (0)1 43 54 81 16
Fax: (0)1 43 26 27 09
E-mail: hotel@rivesdenotredame.com
Web: www.123france.com/notredame

Danièle Limbert &
Christian Martin

Bijou, with just ten rooms. Immense, with the view past *bouquinistes'* stalls to the Seine and the great Cathedral. And perfect soundproofing against the traffic. This is special indeed. The colours and textures of Provence and Tuscany have been brought to an ancient Paris townhouse. There are 17th-century beams, superb 'aged' marble tiling, cupboards delicately painted by a brilliant Tuscan artisan. Light pours in from the glass canopy and the plants rises to meet it. Through an arched 'fortress' door, each bedroom has its own sunny southern materials, all in vibrating colour co-ordinations and contrasts that mix flowers and stars and stripes. Beds have soft luxy duvets and head cushions hanging from wrought-iron ivy-twined rods; each has a pretty bathroom and table and chairs for intimate breakfasts, though the basement breakfast room is intimate and appealing too. Rooms are a good size (just three on the 1st floor are given for singles but could take couples) and the magnificent top-floor studio is huge. The welcome is genuinely friendly and relaxed: your host has time to advise each guest on things to do, and you will feel well cared for in this exceptional house.

Rooms: 10, including 1 junior suite.
Price: Singles & doubles 1100-1750 Frs; suite 2500 Frs (€167.69-266.79).
Breakfast: Continental in room 70 Frs; buffet 90 Frs.
Meals: On request 100-200 Frs.
Metro: St Michel.
RER: St Michel-Notre Dame.
Bus routes: 21 27 38 85 96
Car park: Lutèce.

Those *bouquinistes*, who sell secondhand books of great or minimal value, old magazines and new postcards, are a radical Parisian institution who resist all attempts to 'organise' them.

Map No: 4   **Entry No: 16**

Le Notre Dame Hôtel

1 quai Saint Michel
75005 Paris

Tel: (0)1 43 54 20 43
Fax: (0)1 43 26 61 75

Monsieur Fouhety

If you want to be at the hub of Latin Quarter life, students jostling on the pavements, cars pouring across the Seine, Notre Dame serenely unmovable just there, then climb the mirrored staircase from the noisy embankment to the warm welcome inside. The hotel has been magnificently refurbished, all reception rooms and corridors brightly decked in red checks, the *salon*-breakfast room extended: your eyes are caught by the plunging views of river, Cathedral and great 'police palace'. Nearly all rooms have at least two windows onto this ancient picture; only the five cheapest, soberly pretty and quieter, give onto a dull courtyard. The very attractive rooms are smallish, uncluttered and full of light from the river. Double-glazing keeps the noise out, air conditioning keeps the air breathable. Details: excellent new fabrics by Pierre Frey; light cherry-wood desktops, bedheads and clever block panelling; hand-enamelled bedside lights from northern France and framed prints from England. New dark green marble bathrooms with bright white fittings are extremely smart behind their translucent Japanese-style doors and the top-floor duplex suites are fun and full of character.

Rooms: 26, including 3 duplex.
Price: Singles & doubles 910-1200 Frs (€138.73-182.94); duplex 1500 Frs.
Breakfast: 40 Frs.
Meals: No.
Metro: St Michel.
RER: St Michel-Notre Dame.
Bus routes: 24 47
Car park: Notre Dame.

Run out of bedtime reading? George Whitman's world-famous *Shakespeare & Co*, English-language bookshop and literary meeting place, is just down the road.

Entry No: 17   Map No: 4

 60 Frs

Hôtel Le Clos Médicis

56 rue Monsieur le Prince
75006 Paris

Tel: (0)1 43 29 10 80
Fax: (0)1 43 54 26 90
E-mail: clos_medicis@compuserve.com
Web: www.closmedicis.com

Olivier Méallet

With its stone and glass frontage, the Clos Médicis still looks like the shop it was but the window display is high fashion (red flower pots, green apples and little water-colours when I visited) and coming in from the excited Boulevard St Michel you will hear only muted jazz. Passing an attractive countersunk area with a welcoming (winter) fire, comfy armchairs and a fine stone pillar, you reach the light of the quiet patio and the delightful young team at reception.This place is very contemporary Parisian yet has its roots in provincial soil: a *clos* is a vineyard and each room is named after a famous wine. Bathrooms are impeccable, the tiling brings a whiff of Provence. There are antique-framed pictures and old beams, bold patterns and modern colours, wave-shaped bedheads and tall lampshades, designed by the architect — good reading lights too. Some rooms show a sober, tailored elegance, others are more floral. There's a room with a private terrace, a nicely-arranged duplex. All are soundproofed and, if not always very big, are extremely comfortable. The Beherec family, who also own the Neuville, know how to choose staff who share their lively sense of hospitality.

Rooms: 38.
Price: Singles & doubles 790-1300 Frs
(€120.43-198.18).
Breakfast: Generous buffet 60 Frs.
Meals: No.
Metro: Odéon.
RER: Luxembourg.
Bus routes: 21 38 82 84 85 89
Car park: Rue Soufflot.

The Prince here was a powerful Bourbon who nevertheless had to whisk his bride away from Paris straight after their wedding in 1609 to remove her from King Henri IV's pressing attention.

Map No: 4   **Entry No: 18**

Hôtel de la Sorbonne

6 rue Victor Cousin
75005 Paris

Tel: (0)1 43 54 58 08
Fax: (0)1 40 51 05 18
Web: www.ini.fr/sorbonne.htm

Françoise Testard

The Sorbonne hotel feels like a secret, private hideaway beneath the severe public face of the university. The door is at the back of a wonderful cobbled porchway and the hall huddles shyly behind a great fat pillar. In a quietly confidential atmosphere, an unusual antique kidney-shaped reception desk and a small leather sitting spot await you by the door; the delightful breakfast room beyond has the feel of a country house morning room with its brick-red sponged walls, two bucket chairs beside the marble fireplace, high-backed wicker dining chairs and three African animals in 'aged' sepia ink on the walls to give proper psychological distance. Upstairs, corridors are invigorating and appetising in leaf green and deep raspberry tones. The bedrooms, all being renovated this winter, are not big but things are kept simple and uncluttered. They have white piqué bedcovers and a different colour theme on each floor – mauve or green or blue –, simply-carved wooden bedheads, good-quality mattresses, palely stripey wallpapers and bathrooms in either good contemporary or rather old-fashioned but perfectly adequate tiles; good mirrors too. A quiet, nicely-done hotel in a superb position.

Rooms: 37.
Price: Singles & doubles 520-580 Frs
(€79.27-88.42).
Breakfast: 35 Frs.
Meals: No.
Metro: Cluny-Sorbonne.
RER: Luxembourg.
Bus routes: 21 27 38 63 82 84 86 97
Car park: Rue Soufflot.

The university founded in 1257 by Robert de Sorbon was first called the *Community of Poor Masters and Theological Students*. How times have changed.

Entry No: 19   Map No: 4

Hôtel des Trois Collèges

16 rue Cujas
75005 Paris

Tel: (0)1 43 54 67 30
Fax: (0)1 46 34 02 99

Madame Wyplosz

The open, airy ground floor of the hotel is your breakfast room and, at present, a tea room doing light lunches for all comers. Busy people rush past the big windows but a properly academic atmosphere reigns in the pale and tranquil interior (outside peak hours): the walls are hung with portraits of some great old names of knowledge and with ancient plans showing the Latin Quarter through the ages. This building probably has foundations built when Lutetia was capital of Roman Gaul. In a corner by the lobby, the 22-metre well still holds water: for centuries, it was the sole source of water for all those living round the little courtyard. Bedrooms are simple too with lots of white furniture and pretty pastel-hued piqué bedcovers. The second pillow is dressed up as a cushion on top, there are splashes of colour in the curtains, bathrooms have all the necessary bits plus a clothes line over the bath — so useful. It is a very pleasant and reasonable place to stay right beneath the looming wall of the Sorbonne. Internet access may be available by Easter 2001 but there are plenty of cyber cafés in this young neighbourhood where tomorrow's leaders are still learning their trades.

Rooms: 44.
Price: Singles & doubles 410-730 Frs (€62.50-111.29); extra person 120 Frs.
Breakfast: 45 Frs.
Meals: No.
Metro: St Michel, Odéon.
RER: Luxembourg, Cluny-La Sorbonne.
Bus routes: 21 27 38 63 82 84 86 87
Car park: Rue Soufflot.

Victor Cousin, a daring philosopher who aimed to combine Descartes, Kant and the Scottish school in one great "eclectic" system, left this thought: *It is better to have a future than a past.*

Map No: 4   **Entry No: 20**

Hôtel du Collège de France

7 rue Thénard   **Tel:** (0)1 43 26 78 36
75005 Paris   **Fax:** (0)1 46 34 58 29
                                 E-mail: hotel.du.college.de.france@wanadoo.fr
                                 Web: www.hotel-collegedefrance.com

Jean Marc

Excellent value on a quiet street away from the bustle of the main student drags, this hotel has an atmosphere of solid, well-established family comfort: exposed stones, lots of wood, soft armchairs by the fireplace in the red *salon*, good lighting. You will be greeted by the delightful young manager and by a less animated and considerably older Joan of Arc. The ground-floor breakfast room is warmly red too, with old Parisian prints and a Madonna. Bedrooms are mostly not very big but each has new beds, a full-length mirror and a thoroughly practical desk unit. The décor is quite colourful in places with co-ordinated botanical-theme fabrics, elsewhere there are soft quilts — it is both careful and restful and the bathrooms are fine. Fifth and sixth-floor rooms have balconies on the street side, rooms under the roof have beams and views, even if you have to walk up from the fifth floor. Indeed, the staircase is worth visiting for its round timbers and windows encrusted with autumn leaves. Several triple rooms and family apartments are possible and, above all, a genuinely friendly reception is assured. You may receive useful intellectual vibrations from Le Collège as a bonus.

Rooms: 29.
Price: Singles & doubles 500-550 Frs (€76.22-83.85).
Breakfast: 'Unlimited' Continental 35 Frs.
Meals: No.
Metro: St Michel, Maubert-Mutualité.
RER: St Michel-Notre Dame.
Bus routes: 21 24 27 38 63 85 86 87
Car park: Maubert-Mutualité.

The Collège de France is an astonishing institution: lectures and courses by the greatest teachers and thinkers of the day are open to all, free of charge. *Vive la France!*

Entry No: 21   Map No: 4

Hôtel Minerve

13 rue des Ecoles
75005 Paris

Tel: (0)1 43 26 26 04
Fax: (0)1 44 07 01 96
E-mail: minerve@hotellerie.net

Éric Gaucheron & Sylvie Roger

Éric Gaucheron runs his second hotel (his family started with the Familia next door) with his characteristic energy and eagerness to please: that friendly touch is here too. So is the stimulating university life outside. The newly red-carpeted, creamy-walled corridors lead to rooms that often use the classic, cunning bed alcove for storage space to make up for limited size. The higher you are the longer the view to Notre Dame and the Seine (on the street side of course) — top-floor rooms have some wild and wonderful timbers over their quirky shapes and some rich red, gold and ivory colour schemes. Walls will gradually be decorated with those excellent sepia murals of French monuments, all different. Décor varies from brightly contemporary to soothingly granny, there are damask and satin, timber and tile, some nice old bits of furniture and gilt-framed mirrors, all new beds, some recent built-in cupboards, decent bathrooms that, again, vary in size. The lobby and sitting areas are generously big, light and airy with pleasant repro furniture, tapestries and bookcases. This is a deserving neighbour to the Familia with its long-standing reputation for value and warm-heartedness.

Rooms: 54.
Price: Singles, doubles, triples, quadruples 395-770 Frs (€60.22-117.39).
Breakfast: 37 Frs.
Meals: No.
Metro: Jussieu, Cardinal Lemoine.
RER: Cluny-La Sorbonne.
Bus routes: 47 63 67 86 87
Car park: Lagrange.

Ancient seats of learning: in Rue Cardinal Lemoine, that cleric founded the Collège... Cardinal Lemoine in 1305; in 1332, a priest from Arras opened a school for poor children in... Rue d'Arras.

Map No: 4   Entry No: 22

Familia Hôtel
11 rue des Écoles
75005 Paris

Tel: (0)1 43 54 55 27
Fax: (0)1 43 29 61 77

Éric Gaucheron

It is well named! And its two 'stars' are outshone by the glow of care and attention showered upon house and guests by Éric, his wife Sylvie, their baby son Charles and his parents Bernard and Colette. If the hotel looks grand from the outside with its elaborate balconies, their earnest wish is to welcome you as friends: enthusiastically. Beyond the hall, decorated by an artist friend, is the rich red breakfast/sitting room where the family's collection of leather-bound tomes and the thick oriental rug give a homely feel. This simple atmosphere informs the bedrooms. They are not large or 'Parisian chic' but each has either a mural of a Paris monument, a wall of ancient stones, an old carved bedhead or a balcony onto the fascinating street life — or a mixture of all this. Carpets, wallpapers, bedcovers and curtains seem somehow comfortingly provincial and solid, not brilliantly trendy or stunningly matched. Bedrooms and the small but adequate bathrooms are being renovated and it's all spotless. Front rooms look across the wide street to a rich jumble of old buildings with the Ile Saint Louis just beyond. Ask Éric anything — he will answer willingly, at length and in fast English.

Rooms: 30.
Price: Singles, doubles, triples, quadruples 395-795 Frs (€60.22-121.20).
Breakfast: 35 Frs.
Meals: No.
Metro: Jussieu, Cardinal Lemoine.
RER: Cluny-La Sorbonne.
Bus routes: 47 63 67 86 87
Car park: Lagrange.

This is a typical *Style Noble* 1860s Haussmann building, i.e. it has balconies on 2nd, 5th and 6th floors. Non-nobles lack the 2nd-floor adornment. Look around you for examples.

Entry No: 23   Map No: 4

Hôtel Résidence
Saint Christophe
17 rue Lacépède
75005 Paris

Tel: (0)1 43 31 81 54
Fax: (0)1 43 31 12 54
E-mail:
hotelstchristophe@compuserve.com

Daniel & Jean Robat

 small

The owners of the Saint Christophe — attentive and human people — are entering into their new profession of hotelier with energy and gusto. The hotel, on a quiet street in the old Latin Quarter underneath the Montagne Sainte Geneviève, has a long history of serving the community in various guises and a big attractive sitting room with light flooding in through a wall of window, light that is also enjoyed by two giant plants. A magnificently carved antique armoire is another splendid focus. Upstairs, although the décor is the same in every bedroom, the Robat brothers are making sure that quality reigns. Walls have pinky-yellow sponged wallpaper, bedcovers are quilted in red satiny stuff, bedheads and furniture (minibars included) are Louis XV or Louis XVI, bathrooms are decent in beige marble (some have windows to the outside disconcertingly disguised as mirrors), and the overall atmosphere is of good bourgeois comfort. In the morning, breakfast is served in the white-walled, mirrored basement where upholstered Louis XV chairs and a trompe-l'œil mural of Paris put you in the picture for the day.

Rooms: 31.
Price: Singles & doubles 500-700 Frs (€76.22-106.71).
Breakfast: 50 Frs.
Meals: No.
Metro: Monge.
RER: Gare d'Austerlitz, Luxembourg.
Bus routes: 47 67
Car park: Patriarches.

On its *montagne*, the Pantheon was first dedicated to Geneviève, who saved Paris from Attila the Hun in 451 AD and became the city's patron saint when she died aged 92.

Map No: 4   **Entry No: 24**

Hôtel Résidence Les Gobelins

9 rue des Gobelins
75013 Paris

Tel: (0)1 47 07 26 90
Fax: (0)1 43 31 44 05
E-mail: goblins@cybercable.fr
Web: www.hotelgobelins.com

Jennifer & Philippe Poirier

Street, hotel and owners are quiet, attentive and unassuming; the patio is a real gift. This was a neighbourhood for workers at the great Gobelins tapestry shops and was never very smart but it is near the entertaining, slightly Bohemian Rue Mouffetard with its little eating houses, big mosque, lively market and left-wing intellectual culture. The lounge, with country-cushioned wicker furniture, and the bright yellow, airy breakfast room where a wall of mirrors brings the patio indoors, decorated with much-loved black and white photographs of Paris and Parisians, lie round that honeysuckle-hung courtyard where guests can sit in peace. The rooms and bathrooms are simple, properly equipped — a writing table and chair, a decent cupboard and good towels — and have space (singles are small, of course); décor is yellow, blue and grey, restful and harmonious. All rooms are quiet and light (though party walls may seem rather thin?). The Poiriers' gentle unobtrusive friendliness reminds the sensitive guest that the family used to keep a *pension de famille*; it has kept that incomparable sense of intimacy and understanding.

Rooms: 32.
Price: Singles, doubles, triples 325-555 Frs (€49.55-84.61).
Breakfast: 38 Frs.
Meals: On request 50-150 Frs.
Metro: Gobelins.
RER: Port Royal.
Bus routes: 27 47 83 91
Car park: Place d'Italie.

In 1997, reconstruction works on the other side of the road revealed twelve 5th-century stone sarcophagi containing coffin nails and skeletons, including a child and a horse.

Entry No: 25   **Map No:** 4

Luxembourg – Montparnasse

Hôtel Apollon Montparnasse

91 rue de l'Ouest/54 rue Pernety   **Tel:** (0)1 43 95 62 00
75014 Paris   **Fax:** (0)1 43 95 62 10
                                           E-mail: apollonm@club-internet.fr
                                           Web: www.apollon-montparnasse.fr

Isabelle & Hervé Prigent

The big-windowed, flame-furnished lobby is graced with stripey blinds and a sweet little stone damsel in ancient Greek mode; light pours in from the two streets that meet here — two quietish little streets in this old-style backwater where a slower pace reigns and the metropolitan hubbub seems miles away: there should be little traffic at night. The Prigents named their hotel after meeting Apollo on Mount Parnassus — but have not yet found his stone likeness, even on trips to Greece. And no Ionic scrolls or Corinthian curls either: this is a simple place to stay. Rooms are all furnished in pale laminated wood, clean and neat, with orange-papered walls and either brick-coloured or green and ochre fabrics of excellent contemporary quality. The quilted bedcovers are bright and welcoming, bathrooms are coolly grey and fully equipped and only the single rooms are really small. Also, each room has one or two original prints of figures or abstractions by a talented young artist — a personal touch and a definite focus of interest. Breakfast is in the vaulted basement where discreet lighting and modern furniture set off the old stones. We feel the Apollon is good, sound value.

Rooms: 33.
Price: Singles & doubles 385-480 Frs (€58.69-73.18).
Breakfast: 35 Frs.
Meals: No.
Metro: Pernety.
RER: Denfert Rochereau.
Bus routes: 28 58 68 92
Car park: Consult hotel.

Dom Antoine Pernety was an 18th-century monk who spent years searching for the philosopher's stone and the elixir of eternal life. He died, obviously unsuccessful, a pauper aged 85.

Hôtel Daguerre
94 rue Daguerre
75014 Paris

Tel: (0)1 43 22 43 54
Fax: (0)1 43 20 66 84
E-mail:
hotel.daguerre.paris.14@gofornet.com

Madame Montagnon

In the shadow of the great modern blocks behind Montparnasse there's an area of little streets that feels just like a village and the bottom half of Rue Daguerre is attractively pedestrianised with boutiques and bistrots. The hotel is at the top, motorised, end of the street. It has a certain period grandeur to its public face and a very good breakfast room with the Louvre and pyramid spread across the wall, though the bedrooms are simpler and smaller. Some of them look down into the tiny green patio where ivy climbs the trellises and water flows from the *Boca Veritas* set into the wall; some look over the backyards of other buildings — trees, greenery, quiet — and some, of course, over the street. All are decorated with copies, by a talented artist friend, of one or two famous French paintings; curtains and bedcovers are in smart grey and beige checks and stripes or satiny eastern-type foliage — all quietly acceptable. Space being limited, cupboards may be open-fronted but a couple of rooms have an extra glazed 'balcony' which instantly makes for a much bigger feel. The two suites on the top floor are, of course, bigger and have a nice secluded feel up there. A neat, quiet place for Montparnasse.

Rooms: 30, including 2 suites.
Price: Doubles/suites 500-680 Frs (€76.22-103.67).
Breakfast: Buffet 45 Frs.
Meals: No.
Metro: Gaîté, Denfert Rochereau, Edgar Quinet.
RER: Denfert Rochereau.
Bus routes: 28 38 58 66
Car park: Avenue du Maine.

Daguerre, whose discovery of how to fix images laid the ground for photography, was a patriot, preferring to bequeath his system to France and refusing riches offered him by foreigners.

Map No: 4   **Entry No: 27**

Hôtel Istria

29 rue Campagne Première
75014 Paris

Tel: (0)1 43 20 91 82
Fax: (0)1 43 22 48 45

Daniel Crétey

50 Frs

You will receive a genuinely warm welcome from Daniel Crétey at the Istria which is superbly placed for transport from airports, stations and the attractions of lively Montparnasse, yet secluded in a quiet back street. A haunt of the wild arty set who lived, loved and worked here in the heyday of the 1930s avant-garde, the hotel now promises peace and quiet with its deep leather sofas while celebrity takes the shape of a small wooden Charlie Chaplin sitting benignly in the corner. Plain, simple, good-quality furnishings and décor are the hallmark: the contemporary bedroom furniture made of gently-curved pieces of solid elm, specially designed for the Istria by Jacques Athenor, is enlivened with fine-checked or striped fabrics and heavy stainless steel table lamps. The same discreet, simple taste prevails in the palest yellow Korean grass wallpaper. The showers (there are four baths in all) are delightful quarter-circle constructions while beds have slatted bases and firm new Dunlopillo mattresses. In the lovely stone-vaulted breakfast room soft lighting lifts the scattered yellow and orange flowers from the tablecloths. Charm and thoroughly good value for two stars near Montparnasse.

Rooms: 26.
Price: Singles & doubles 580-650 Frs (€88.42-99.09).
Breakfast: Continental plus 50 Frs.
Meals: On request about 100 Frs.
Metro: Raspail.
RER: Port-Royal.
Bus routes: 68 91
Car park: Montparnasse.

The Istria was immortalised by Louis Aragon in a poem to his beloved Elsa; Duchamp invented his 'readymade' art here; Man Ray took pictures — glory enough?

Entry No: 28   Map No: 4

Hôtel Aiglon

232 boulevard Raspail
75014 Paris

Tel: (0)1 43 20 82 42
Fax: (0)1 43 20 98 72
E-mail: hotelaiglon@wanadoo.fr

Jacques Rols

Built over a smart brasserie, the Aiglon is a three-star plus, spaces are generous, the imperial eagle everywhere: Empire furniture, even an Empire lift, beside which trickles the stream of a delicious little rockery. In the Empire bar, those fine books hide bottles. The next delight is the large, light mahogany-panelled breakfast room over the trees. All rooms have a lobby, walk-in cupboard and custom-made furniture (beds, chairs, chest-cum-minibar); mostly big by Paris standards, they are supremely restful. Colours are green with yellow, or deep beige with muted multi-coloured prints; fine table lamps by Drimmer and watercolours add grace; firm new mattresses guarantee comfort. Light-tiled bathrooms are well equipped: even the small shower rooms have proper-sized stalls. Many rooms give onto tree-lined avenues whence most traffic disappears at night, and some bathe in the green peace of the cemetery. The superb de luxe suite, is imperially vast, its minibar has little columns. But the welcome is by no means haughtily Empire or powerfully Napoleonic. People stay for weeks, come again and become friends of this warm family. *Internet access on ground floor.*

Rooms: 42, including 9 suites.
Price: Singles & doubles 510-870 Frs
(€77.75-132.63); suites 1090-1520 Frs.
Breakfast: 40 Frs.
Meals: No.
Metro: Raspail.
RER & Orlybus: Denfert Rochereau.
Bus routes: 68 91
Car park: Hotel or Edgar Quinet.

Napoleon's son and heir, nicknamed *Aiglon* (Little Eagle), died at 21 and never carried the Imperial insignia. The hotel's previous owner was an ardent fan of Napoleon.

Map No: 4   **Entry No: 29**

Hôtel Raspail Montparnasse

203 boulevard Raspail
75014 Paris

Tel: (0)1 43 20 62 86
Fax: (0)1 43 20 50 79
E-mail: raspailm@aol.com

Madame Christiane Martinent

The frontage is deliciously, authentically 1924, until you step up to those heavy old doors and they spring open — modern magic. 'The best of old and new' is the theme here. Inside, the old-style generosity is again apparent in the high-ceilinged Art Deco lobby with its bucket chairs, wood panelling and play of squares and curves. The custom-designed bedroom furniture, 1930s or modern, sits well with pale unfussy quilts, pretty lamps and an extremely elegant curtain material. To each floor a colour: quiet, relaxing grey, sunny ochre, powder-puff blue; to each landing a 'matching' stained glass window — good later additions to the original 1924 framework. Obviously, the higher the price, the larger the room, but even the 'Standard Double' has a decent desk and an armchair while 'Superiors' are most attractive. Bathrooms are stylishly white-tiled and colour-friezed with smart matt washbasins. Each room is named after one of the famous Montparnasse artists and decorated with an appropriate print; some have the added perk of an Eiffel Tower view. A friendly and efficient welcome is the final flourish. *NB Don't confuse it with the Mercure Raspail Montparnasse two doors down!*

Rooms: 38, including 2 junior suites.
Price: Singles & doubles 590-990 Frs (€89.94-150.92); suites 1300 Frs.
Breakfast: 50 Frs.
Meals: No.
Metro: Vavin, Raspail.
RER: Port Royal.
Bus routes: 58 68 82 91
Car park: Montparnasse-Raspail.

That statue of Balzac, author of the immense *Comédie Humaine*, by the equally famous sculptor Rodin, shocked contemporaries who saw it as "a madman in his dressing-gown".

Entry No: 30   Map No: 4

Pension Les Marronniers

78 rue d'Assas
75006 Paris

Tel: (0)1 43 26 37 71
Fax: (0)1 43 26 07 72
E-mail: o_marro@club-internet.fr
Web: www.pension-marronniers.com

Marie Poirier

This may be your last chance! The genuine *pension de famille* is a threatened species so if you're young and penniless or old and nostalgic, make the most of Marie's quintessentially French family flat (and its annexes) overlooking the Luxembourg Gardens. A *pension* since the 1900s (her parents ran it before her), it is as personal and cluttered as any description from Balzac. There are innumerable pictures, portraits and photographs, there are statues and plants galore, notices for *pensionnaires* on flower pots and mantelpieces, a cuckoo clock that has stopped and a superbly-carved, grass-green country armoire topped with a motley crew of candlesticks. Marie loves her guests (one has been here for 24 years) and loves cooking for them: she clearly enjoys food herself and will make sure others do too. She is down-to-earth, compassionate, perceptive and hard-working — a remarkable woman. The bedrooms for short-stayers have less personality than the dining and drawing rooms, rather as if they have been furnished with what was left over, and most share washing facilities. But what counts is the wonderful welcome, the tradition and the food. *Reductions for long stays.*

Rooms: 12, some with own shower & wc, some sharing.
Price: 170-395 Frs (€25.92-60.22) half-board; extra person 100 Frs.
Breakfast: Included.
Meals: Dinner included (lunch on Saturdays, cold supper on Sundays).
Metro: Notre Dame des Champs, Vavin. **RER:** Luxembourg.
Bus routes: 58 84
Car park: Rue Auguste Comte.

Legend has it that Captain Assas of the Auvergne Chasseurs, searching a wood alone one night, was taken by the enemy and died saving his comrades with the cry *"A moi, Auvergne!"*.

Map No: 4

Entry No: 31

 small

Le Sainte Beuve

9 rue Sainte-Beuve
75006 Paris

Tel: (0)1 45 48 20 07
Fax: (0)1 45 48 67 52
E-mail: saintebeuve@wanadoo.fr
Web: www.paris-hotel-charme.com

Jean-Pierre Egurreguy

Designer flair pervades this beautifully-refurbished hotel, known and loved during the wilder days of Montparnasse but now very quiet. The atmosphere is of light, unstuffy luxury — quiet good taste in gentle tones and thick furnishings (superb gold and ivory silk curtains). In winter a log fire burns in the old marble fireplace and clients often take a drink from the bar to one of the deeply embracing sofas. The attentive efficient staff are a vital element in your sense of well-being here. It is small and intimate, and so are the bedrooms. The general tone is ancient and modern: lots of white walls, soft colours and contemporary textured fabrics, the pastels modulated by more colourful chintzes and paisleys, at least one antique per room — a leather-topped desk, a walnut dressing-table, a polished armoire — and 19th-century pictures in rich old frames. The *Sainte Beuve* suite is extra-big, in dazzling good taste and very special. Superbly modern bathrooms have bathrobes and fine toiletries. Lastly, for the first moments of the day, breakfast is a feast of croissants and brioches from the famous Mulot bakery and fresh orange juice. *Book early.*

Rooms: 22, including 1 junior suite.
Price: Singles & doubles 780-1700 Frs (€118.91-259.16); suite 1950 Frs.
Breakfast: 85 Frs.
Meals: On request 40-200 Frs.
Metro: Notre Dame des Champs, Vavin.
RER: Port Royal.
Bus routes: 48 58 82 89 91 94 95 96
Car Park: Montparnasse.

Moral philosopher and literary critic, Sainte Beuve was known for his *bons mots* such as "The historian is a prophet of the past", "So many die before meeting themselves".

Entry No: 32

Map No: 4

Hôtel Le Saint Grégoire

43 rue de l'Abbé Grégoire
75006 Paris

Tel: (0)1 45 48 23 23
Fax: (0)1 45 48 33 95
E-mail: hotel@saintgregoire.com
Web: www.hotelsaintgregoire.com

Michel Bouvier, Lucie Agaud & François de Bené

The tall slim façade of the Saint-Grégoire looks even more 18th-century elegant when compared to the uglies on the other side of the street. Inside, the elegance is more contemporary: deep comfortable chairs, Indian rugs on fitted carpets and a colour scheme designed by David Hicks in plum, old pink and ginger, a red doormat, a brass-ringed half-curtain, a simple classical fireplace (fires in winter) — and there is a friendly, attentive and intelligent welcome and four-star plushness. We love the atmosphere in the little reading room with its gentle classical music and antiques lovingly collected by the owners. In one terrace bedroom, you will find a set of intriguing folding coathooks, in the other, an unusual thickset writing desk that bears witness to serious work done. Room sizes vary, the larger ones look over the street, some with two windows, but every one has a genuinely old piece or two. Pinks, browns and white are the colours, including bathroom marble, and there are pretty rugs strewn everywhere, but breakfast on one of the two private terraces is perhaps the tops. Serene, intimate and remarkably French, it is linked to the larger Tourville and Lavoisier hotels.

Rooms: 20, including 1 suite & 2 terrace rooms.
Price: Singles & doubles 890-1090 Frs (€135.68-166.17), terrace rooms 1490 Frs.
Breakfast: Continental plus 70 Frs.
Meals: No.
Metro: St Placide, Sèvres-Babylone.
RER: Luxembourg.
Bus routes: 63 68 84 89 92 94
Car park: Opposite hotel.

Abbé Grégoire, a revolutionary bishop: he proposed ending the feudal Right of Primogeniture (eldest boy takes all), and in 1794 persuaded France to abolish slavery.

Map No: 4

Entry No: 33

Hôtel Ferrandi

92 rue du Cherche-Midi
75006 Paris

Tel: (0)1 42 22 97 40
Fax: (0)1 45 44 89 97
E-mail: hotel.ferrandi@wanadoo.fr

Madame Lafond

Behind the harmonious spread of the frontage (every room looks this way), you will find a cheerful, friendly and efficient team and a superb demonstration of old-style French refinement. Some of the beautiful antiques in the *salon* are family pieces, each fabric, flounce and swag has been carefully planned, the club-like breakfast room is properly intimate behind its screen of greenery and the 1920s posters, prints and drawings have been lovingly chosen to delight your eye at every turn. Enter the smallest, cosiest room: a deeply tempting dark blue and white nest lined with quiet scenes of Ancient Greece and enfolding a pure white brass-headed bed set in a soft ivory alcove with every detail perfect. The very generous deluxe rooms are variously decked in wine red, rich blue or salmon pink Jouy prints of romantic country scenes with matching plush chairs and a big desk each. Curtains are luxuriously thick, bathrooms dressed in marble slabs or good tiles. Other careful details: thorough soundproofing, excellent tap fittings, interactive film/TV system. You know they want you to feel absolutely at home in this place of rich peace and proper comfort.

Rooms: 42, including 1 suite.
Price: Singles & doubles 620-1480 Frs (€94.52-225.62).
Breakfast: Continental plus 65 Frs.
Meals: No.
Metro: Vaneau, St Placide.
RER: Luxembourg, St Michel-Notre Dame.
Bus routes: 39 95 48 82 68 70
Car park: Ask at hotel.

The street was named in 1595. In the 16th century, a *cherche-midi* was a social parasite who made a habit of visiting at midday in the hope of being invited to lunch.

Entry No: 34   Map No: 3

St Germain des Prés – Orsay

Grand Hôtel des Balcons
3 rue Casimir Delavigne
75006 Paris

Tel: (0)1 46 34 78 50
Fax: (0)1 46 34 06 27
Web: www.balcons.com

Denise & Pierre Corroyer
& Jeff

Yes, it is balconied, and moulded, and corniced. But the real originality is in the Art Nouveau interior. Denise Corroyer took the original 1890s staircase windows — irises, lilies and bindweed — and copied their voluptuous curves onto panels, screens and lights. She now teaches *ikebana* and flowers the hotel — brilliantly. Jeff, her son and hotel manager, is enthusiastic about their philosophy of service which produces tea and coffee on winter afternoons, a clothes line over the bath and a practical, modern meeting room where clients can work or children play. Owners and staff all appear to work with lightness and pleasure. There are now five big new family rooms with smart décor and pretty modern lamps, parquet floors and two windows, good bathrooms (two basins, pretty tiles) and loads of space. Other rooms are not big but purpose-made table units use the space judiciously, amusing prints decorate the walls and front rooms have... balconies. At the back, you may be woken by the birds. An eagle eye is kept and no damage left unrepaired, beds are firm, bathrooms good, colours and fabrics simple and pleasantly bright. And breakfast — a feast every day — is FREE on your birthday!

Rooms: 50, including 5 family rooms.
Price: Singles & doubles 435-830 Frs (€66.32-126.53).
Breakfast: Superb buffet 59 Frs.
Meals: No.
Metro: Odéon.
RER: Luxembourg.
Bus routes: 24 63 86 87 96
Car park: Ecole de Médecine.

The classical-fronted Odéon, Second National Theatre 150 years ago, shut down in 1968 for allowing student revolutionaries to hold rallies there, is again sagely part of the Comédie Française.

Entry No: 35

Map No: 4

Hôtel Louis II

2 rue Saint-Sulpice
75006 Paris

Tel: (0)1 46 33 13 80
Fax: (0)1 46 33 17 29
E-mail: louis2@club-internet.fr

François Meynant

Imagination has triumphed in this charming 18th-century house, often to dramatic effect (how about pink satin bamboo wallpaper in the loo?), so that even the smallest rooms (some tight, with little storage) have huge personality. Two have dazzling wraparound trompe-l'œil pictures set into the timber frame. On the top floor, sleep under ancient sloping roof timbers in a long flower-papered room where lace bedcovers are so fitting and there's an old rustic armoire or a 1920s cheval glass. One bathroom has brass taps and a yellow cockleshell basin, the other has an oval bath and burnished copper fittings. Every room is different, sheets are floral in colours to match the décor, bath/shower rooms are small but fully equipped. Next morning, eat a generous and refined breakfast in the newly-clothed golden elegance of the big *salon* with its magnificent fanning beams (and superb new double-sided curtains!). Gilt-framed mirrors, fine antiques and candelabras complete the picture. You will be enthusiastically welcomed by manager and staff and properly cared for: attention to detail is essential and they tend to treat guests like visiting friends.

Rooms: 22.
Price: Singles & doubles 640-980 Frs (€97.57-149.40); triples 1200 Frs; child under 3 free.
Breakfast: Continental plus 70 Frs.
Meals: No.
Metro: Odéon.
RER: St Michel-Notre Dame.
Bus routes: 63 87 86 96 58 70
Car park: St Sulpice.

Prince Louis II was the Grand Condé who fought so brilliantly first against then for Sun King Louis XIV then retired in peace and wealth to Chantilly, surrounded by great writers and poets.

Map No: 4   Entry No: 36

Hôtel du Globe
15 rue des Quatre-Vents
75006 Paris

Tel: (0)1 46 33 62 69/
     (0)1 43 26 35 50
Fax: (0)1 46 33 62 69

Simonne Ressier

Closed in August. Miniature is the word, for the hotel, the rooms, the staircase, the storage, but huge are the hearts of the small team who run it. They simply adore their little hostelry, put fresh flowers in your room and want only that you adore it too. Greet the iron man, walk up the stairs and you will find the *Réception*: a sitting room full of furniture and papers and no office equipment. You are in someone's house and they welcome you with a smile rather than a form to fill in. Bedcovers are grandmotherly lace, there are beams, old stones and four-posters, pink rooms and yellow rooms, little carved *guéridon* tables, tiny folding writing tables and dozens more personal pieces; even the drinks list in your room is hand written. No two rooms are alike. The smallest have shower, basin and loo neatly hidden behind doors that would be plain cupboards if they weren't hand-painted by a skilful artist. Rooms with baths are larger — one on the ground floor has its own tiny patio — and wherever you sleep you also have breakfast. For character, charm and warmth of welcome, the Globe is hard to beat. But do take your earplugs in case you are in a streetside (disco-side) room.

Rooms: 15.
Price: Singles & doubles 545-655 Frs
(€83.08-99.85).
Breakfast: 50 Frs.
Meals: No.
Metro: Odéon.
RER: Cluny-La Sorbonne.
Bus routes: 86 87
Car park: St Sulpice.

In the 17th century, the four winds (*quatre vents*) blew to the four corners of the earth from the round cheeks and delicious lips of four cherubs — on a shop sign.

Entry No: 37   Map No: 4

Hôtel de l'Odéon
13 rue Saint Sulpice
75006 Paris

Tel: (0)1 43 25 70 11
Fax: (0)1 43 29 97 34
E-mail: hotel.de.lodeon@wanadoo.fr
Web: www.hoteldelodeon.com

Monsieur & Madame Pilfert

The pretty Parisian façade deceives: enter and discover the most unexpected feast of space, elegance, oak panelling and attention to detail round a delicious green and flowery corner. The Pilferts' collection of antique beds would make any collector envious — maybe a canopied four-poster (or two), or a pair of elaborately decorated cast-iron beds, even incorporating a couple of figures. You will have crochet bedcovers, a nice old mirror and a window onto the narrow street or greenery. Beams abound, carefully-co-ordinated colour schemes mean quiet traditional comfort and bathrooms are marble. The owner has used his ingenuity and sense of architectural volumes to make even the small rooms feel special (e.g. two windows cantilevered out over the patio transforming a narrow single room into a real space). Wherever feasible, those antique bedsteads have been adapted to take extra-wide mattresses. The generous breakfast is in the 'garden room' that gives onto that lovely little patio with its creepers, flowers and figurines, or in the soft sitting area beside the handmade, antique-fitted glass telephone box — quite a feature. The Odéon is quiet and friendly and there's room to move.

Rooms: 30.
Price: Singles & doubles 830-1350 Frs (€126.53-205.81); family rooms 1450-1550 Frs.
Breakfast: Continental plus 65 Frs.
Meals: No.
Metro: Odéon.
RER: St Michel-Notre Dame.
Bus routes: 21 27 38 58 82 84 85 89
Car park: St Sulpice.

The secular astronomical Gnomon in St Sulpice catches sunlight from a hole in the wall, projects it onto the brass line inlaid in the floor and thus announces equinoxes and solstices.

Map No: 4   **Entry No: 38**

Welcome Hôtel

66 rue de Seine
75006 Paris

Tel: (0)1 46 34 24 80
Fax: (0)1 40 46 81 59
Web: www.welcomehotel-paris.com

Monsieur Henneveux, Perrine Henneveux

On the corner of Rue de Seine and Boulevard St Germain, in the middle of one of the trendiest parts of Paris where the delightful Rue de Buci street market and the legendary St Germain cafés meet, the Welcome has that comfortable atmosphere created by a natural and unpretentious attitude to life and people. The ground-floor reception is tiny but there's a bit more space as you move up towards the light. On the first floor is the small, timbered, tapestried, Louis XIII-furnished *salon* which looks down onto the bustle below. And most bedrooms are smallish. They are all different and all give onto one or other of the streets so you will be grateful for efficient double glazing. The variegated décor is being freshened up with new bright contemporary fabrics instead of the present 'Andean' or tapestry bedcovers and multi-styled wallpapers: there's already a smart new bottle green carpet and bathrooms are being prettily tiled. Top-floor rooms have sloping ceilings and beams, one is reached through its half-timbered bathroom! A couple have great views across the treetops and the boulevard; it's quirky, a wee bit scruffy for the moment, but absolutely in the thick of things.

Rooms: 30.
Price: Singles, doubles, triples 435-735 Frs (€66.32-112.05).
Breakfast: 50 Frs.
Meals: No.
Metro: St Germain des Prés, Mabillon, Odéon.
RER: St Michel-Notre Dame.
Bus routes: 39 48 58 63 70 86 87 95
Car park: St Germain des Prés, St Sulpice.

On the corner of Rue de Seine and Rue de Buci is a café with delightfully relaxed young staff who serve coffee as it was done 'in the old days': with vanilla — and a smile.

Entry No: 39 Map No: 4

Hôtel de Seine

52 rue de Seine   **Tel:** (0)1 46 34 22 80
75006 Paris   **Fax:** (0)1 46 34 04 74
                                         Web: www.hotel-de-seine.com

Monsieur Henneveux, Perrine Henneveux

Underneath the arches, through the big wooden doors, and you enter what once was, and still feels like, a private mansion; the welcome from the delightful staff adds to this impression. Two really French *salons*, with fresh flowers, space and deep quiet, lead off the hall. In deference to guests' different tastes, the breakfast room, presided over by a delicate little Pan, has a large table for the sociable and several small tables for the less so; walls are clothed in Florentine-style fabric, chairs are blue and studded, antique corner cupboards glow. Bedrooms have similar class with their strong, complementary colour schemes, gently painted Louis XVI or highly polished, cane-seated Directoire furniture and, again, that sense of being in a family home not an anonymous hotel. One room displays a rather daring use of black paint and gilt edging in honour of the 1850s craze for all things Far Eastern; others have quirky layouts dictated by the old architecture. Elegant marble bathrooms are much mirrored and the higher floors naturally carry 18th-century timbers and the occasional balcony for rooftop views or birds-eye vistas of fine Parisian façades. A good place to stay.

Rooms: 30.
Price: Singles, doubles, triples 775-1190 Frs (€118.15-181.41).
Breakfast: 65 Frs.
Meals: No.
Metro: St Germain des Prés, Mabillon, Odéon.
RER: St Michel-Notre Dame.
Bus routes: 39 48 58 63 70 86 87 95
Car park: Mazarine.

Francis Ford Coppola used to have reels of film delivered openly to the Crillon (Paris's most exclusive palace hotel) while he stayed incognito at the somewhat simpler Seine.

Map No: 4   **Entry No: 40**

Hôtel Saint André des Arts

66 rue Saint-André-des-Arts
75006 Paris

Tel: (0)1 43 26 96 16
Fax: (0)1 43 29 73 34
E-mail: hsaintand@minitel.net

Henri & Odile Le Goubin

The old shop front of this relaxed, low-cost hotel beside the bustling St André crossroads has been known and loved by backpackers and intellectuals for years. You enter to a row of old choir stalls, a listed staircase and Henri, a former philosophy teacher who is happy to talk *philo* and Proust with them, not the latest in design. But the old coconut matting has gone from the walls! White paint sets off the old timbers, new carpets are on their way, all windows are new and double-glazed, new little tiled shower rooms are being fitted. Still, nothing can ever hide how the building twists and turns round the courtyard. Some rooms are very small, one is reached across an interior balcony. Some have immensely high ceilings and great windows, beams, old stone walls, 16th-century style. Practical Rustic French antique furniture is set in a simple, pleasant décor. Breakfast is in the reception area at a wonderful great 'folding' table set on a trompe-l'œil black and white floor that was laid 200 years ago. The neighbourhood is lively, the music sometimes noisy and nocturnal, the atmosphere stimulating. If you feel you would like to join in, book early — it's often full.

Rooms: 31.
Price: Single, double, triple, quadruple, including breakfast, 400-680 Frs (€60.98-103.67).
Breakfast: Included.
Meals: No.
Metro: Odéon.
RER: St Michel-Notre Dame.
Bus routes: 63 70 86 87 96
Car park: Rue Mazarine.

'Arts' really means 'arcs' (bows, as in arrows): this was the arms merchants' district. Two muskets discovered on the old hotel wall betray the origins of the old house.

Entry No: 41   Map No: 4

Hôtel d'Aubusson

33 rue Dauphine
75006 Paris

Tel: (0)1 43 29 43 43
Fax: (0)1 43 29 12 62
E-mail: reservationherve@hoteldaubusson.com
Web: www.hoteldaubusson.com

Pascal Gimel

The narrow street is busy, almost frantic at times — but pass the superb old doors into the flagstoned hall, breath in the space, hear the quiet piano from the Café Laurent bar, see the promise of magnificence through the glass patio doors: you have changed centuries. It is an absolutely beautiful stone building, serene and elegant in its golden 17th-century proportions, properly up to date in its 1996 renovation. Reading by the vast stone fireplace (log fires in winter) in the antique-furnished *salon* or breakfasting in the (naturally) Aubusson-tapestried room beyond, you are enveloped in pure French style: densely-beamed ceilings five metres over your head, tall slim windows, superb Versailles parquet floors. There are two lovely patios, the luxurious bar on the street side and a Louis XVI Internet point in a quiet corner. Most bedrooms are big, some very big, some with wonderful beams, all richly furnished in modern/traditional custom-made mahogany, thick quiet-hued fabrics (grey-green, wine-red, ochre, dark blue, ivory), white and grey bathrooms (not huge but with all requisites). This is a peaceful house and much care is taken of guests at all times.

Rooms: 50, including 3 duplex.
Price: Singles, doubles, suites 1300-2300 Frs (€198.18-350.63).
Breakfast: 110 Frs & à la carte.
Meals: Light meals at hotel's Café Laurent: menu 220 Frs & à la carte.
Metro: Odéon.
RER: St Michel-Notre Dame.
Bus routes: 56 63 70 86 87 96
Car park: At hotel.

The hotel's logo is the coat of arms of the town of Aubusson ("she blooms among thorns") where the famous 17th-century Royal Tapestry Factory wove its renowned foliage pictures.

Hôtel de Nesle

7 rue de Nesle
75006 Paris

Tel: (0)1 43 54 62 41
Fax: (0)1 43 54 31 88

Madame Busillet & David Busillet

Backpackers' hostel *extraordinaire* and NOT an hotel for clean towels daily, great storage and silence by 10.30pm. There is none other like it and no other owner like Madame Renée, the lovable matron who, with son David, rules her young visitors with *bonhomie*. Old furniture and dried flowers give the *salon* a carefree atmosphere — a collection of old Larousses adds a serious touch. And on the first floor — an astonishing garden: roses, apricot trees and pond; half the rooms give onto it, many of them carrying David's bright French colonial frescoes. Try *Afrique* for French explorers and mosquito-netted bed, *Sahara* for a private patio and hammam, or *Ancienne* for old photographs and lace. All individually furnished with *brocante* and pretty mirrors, soft modern colours and great charm, rooms are spotlessly clean with good mattresses. BUT, even if the price suits and the old beams please, the facilities may be too scant for your comfort: virtually no storage, one shower (magnificent in dark green marble with romantic broken column) for 10 rooms and NO booking: ring or come in the morning for the evening... and enjoy the warm friendliness. *Sharing possible.*

Rooms: 10 with shower & wc; 10 with basin, sharing 1 shower & 4 wcs.
Price: Singles & doubles 325-650 Frs (€49.55-99.09); extra bed 75 Frs.
Breakfast: Not available.
Meals: No.
Metro: Odéon.
RER: St Michel-Notre Dame.
Bus routes: 58 63 70 86 87 96
Car park: Rue Mazarine.

The Tower of Nesle was (in)famous for housing princesses who seduced and 'used' handsome young men then threw them into the river to conceal their own depravities.

Entry No: 43 Map No: 2 & 4

L'Hôtel
13 rue des Beaux Arts
75006 Paris

Tel: (0)1 44 41 99 00
Fax: (0)1 43 25 64 81
E-mail: reservation@l-hotel.com
Web: www.l-hotel.com

Fabienne Cappelli

Astonishing! Dare I say unique? Your eyes are drawn up, up, up that inimitable central well, past marble pilasters and medallioned galleries to the light. The only hotel to call itself The Hotel has been fabulously renovated by Jacques Garcia with due respect for its neo-Classical origins, for music-hall star Mistinguett (her outrageously glamorous all-mirrors bedroom still stands) and for Oscar Wilde (he died an exiled pauper here). Jorge Luis Borgès, who had quarters here, now has a library corner and *Le Cardinal* has, naturally, the biggest, lushest, luxiest top-floor gold and cardinal-red suite with its own terrace. The *Charles X* suite is softly restful in pale gold Regency stripes with a touch of purple in carpet and bathroom. Other rooms, all on strikingly different themes, are a lot smaller but huge in character and all now have rich marble-alcove bathrooms. The dining room? Under a great glass canopy, it is a riot of stucco work and plush furnishings with a little patio beyond where the lovely old fountain sings. A charming young manageress and a mass of genuine antiques, pictures and *objets*, make this a place for connoisseurs of taste and comfort.

Rooms: 20.
Price: Singles, doubles, suites 1800-4300 Frs (€274.41-655.53).
Breakfast: 110 Frs.
Meals: On request 100-300 Frs. Restaurant opening shortly.
Metro: St Germain des Prés.
RER: St Michel-Notre Dame, Châtelet-Les Halles. **Bus routes:** 39 48 95
Car park: Rue Mazarine.

Borgès, expected by Mitterand for the Legion of Honour, was late, yet he offered to autograph books for FMR bookshop clients opposite: "But you're late for the President, Monsieur Borgès!" "One is always late for someone."

Millésime Hôtel
15 rue Jacob
75006 Paris

Tel: (0)1 44 07 97 97
Fax: (0)1 46 34 55 97
E-mail: reservation@millesimehotel.cc
Web: www.millesimehotel.com

Robert Leclercq

 small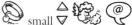

There cannot be a friendlier, warmer welcome in the whole of St Germain! Behind its vast and imposing old wooden doors, the Millésime is intimate and pretty, offering big smiles that more than make up for the smallness of the lobby. The colour mix has a warm southern aura with its brick red and soft yellow ingredients. You first meet these in the deep sofas set on glowing parquet beyond reception. From here, the charming little patio is visible with its plants and tables — three of the rooms are reached from the patio itself. This is a fine old building and the new owners have restored the 17th-century staircase with proper respect, despite the lift in the middle: it's worth a visit. Bedrooms, which vary in size but are never cramped, have pale yellow walls and good white and grey bathrooms. There are a variety of cast-iron lamps whose ancient look contrasts with the pretty, contemporary checks and stripes that cover beds and windows, and unusual wood-backed pictures of formal gardens hang on walls; two top-floor rooms have brilliant high-peaked ceilings and roof windows over historic towers and domes. Altogether eminently attractive.

Rooms: 22.
Price: Singles & doubles 950-1250 Frs
(€144.83-190.56).
Breakfast: Continental in room 75 Frs;
buffet 95 Frs.
Meals: No.
Metro: St Germain des Prés.
RER: St Michel-Notre Dame.
Bus routes: 39 48 63 86 95
Car park: St Germain des Prés.

At the end of Rue de Seine, just before the archway to the river, is a quiet little garden dedicated to Champollion, decipherer of the Egyptian hieroglyphs and a national hero.

Entry No: 45

Map No: 2 & 4

Hôtel des Marronniers

21 rue Jacob
75006 Paris

Tel: (0)1 43 25 30 60
Fax: (0)1 40 46 83 56
Web: www.hotel-marronniers.com

Monsieur Henneveux, Perrine Henneveux

With its real garden, this is another of the Henneveux private mansion hotels. The courtyard entrance (notice the ineffably Parisian *concierge's* lodge on the left) promises peace but not dramatic style. Surprise: the grandiose Empire *salon*, all ruched drapes and gilt, leads to a delicious conservatory where red-cushioned iron chairs and marble-topped tables wait for you under fruity 'chandeliers' and, beyond, a shrubby garden. A privilege indeed. Room sizes vary: mostly smallish, they all give onto the garden or the front courtyard so no need for double glazing. From the top floor you see higgledy-piggledy rooftops or the church tower; from all rooms you hear the chimes. The décor is based on co-ordinated fabrics (some beds have canopies), bright floral prints or Regency stripes serving as backdrop to an antique desk, a carved armoire or a pair of lemon-tree spray lights. Lots of character here. Recently-renovated bathrooms are most attractive, be they grey and ginger marble or white tiles with an original tropical island 'picture'. After so much light, the basement breakfast room is in soft, dark contrast for cool winter mornings. Or opt for the conservatory.

Rooms: 37.
Price: Singles, doubles, triples 650-1220 Frs (€99.09-185.99).
Breakfast: Buffet 70 Frs.
Meals: No.
Metro: St Germain des Prés.
RER: St Michel-Notre Dame.
Bus routes: 39 48 63 86 95
Car park: St Germain des Prés.

Strangely, this street bears Jacob's name because Queen Margot, Catholic wife of Protestant-turned-Catholic King Henri IV, built a shrine to the Jewish patriarch here.

 som‹

Hôtel des Deux Continents

25 rue Jacob
75006 Paris

Tel: (0)1 43 26 72 46
Fax: (0)1 43 25 67 80
E-mail: continents.hotel@wanadoo.fr
Web: www.2continents-hotel.com

Monsieur Henneveux, Perrine Henneveux

Hotels, interior decorators and antique shops jostle for space here so don't miss the discreet entrance to the Deux Continents and its three ancient, listed buildings. The ground-floor public rooms are atmospherically heavy with beams, gilt frames, draperies and dark furniture, lightened at the front by the big street window and at the back by a little patio. Venus stands shyly among the greenery and tables are laid with fine white cloths and bright china against a green and gold backdrop. The geography is intriguing: two buildings look onto quiet inner courtyards, the front building has the larger but noisier rooms. They are done in contemporary-classic style with lots of fabric — walls, bedheads, covers, curtains, pelmets, the odd canopy — in occasionally surprising mixtures of colours and patterns; but it all 'works', as do the bronze lights and pretty old mirrors. The smallest rooms, in the last building (two storeys, no lift), are utterly quiet, equally charming and air-conditioned. Some rooms have rooftop views, some look onto flowered terraces. The whole place has masses of personality, the staff are young and welcoming and you are ideally placed for St Germain des Prés.

Rooms: 41.
Price: Singles, doubles, triples 795-1120 Frs (€121.20-170.74).
Breakfast: 65 Frs.
Meals: No.
Metro: St Germain des Prés.
RER: St Michel-Notre Dame.
Bus routes: 39 48 63 86 95
Car park: St Germain des Prés.

Which two continents? The Old World and the New. In 1783 America and Great Britain signed the Treaty of Independence in a house just a few blocks down from here.

Entry No: 47   Map No: 4

La Villa
29 rue Jacob
75006 Paris

Tel: (0)1 43 26 60 00
Fax: (0)1 46 34 63 63
E-mail: hotel@villa-saintgermain.com
Web: www.villa-saintgermain.com

Christine Horbette

The lobby/lounge/bar is so perfectly St Germain des Près, you know you have 'arrived'. Soberly studied forms and colours: big blocky black desk, curvy steel stair rail, soft sleek grey silk curtains, big ochre-flecked stone floor slabs; gentle jazz and a smiling ever-present barman (or so it seemed). By the bar, a series of deep, plush chairs in grey, brown and beige on a teak floor. Staff are young, bright and attentive. The new owners are renovating all the rooms: still fairly small for their four stars, except the junior suites, they are definitely still contemporary but less extravagantly so. The drama of colour is now red, black and white, the gentleness will be ivory and moss green, all modulated by Regency fashion plates. Materials are rich and yielding — thick blue curtains folded back on fine silk linings, 'crocodile'-skin bedheads in black wooden frames, fluffy white duvets with dark grey and ivory woollen squares on top, all against a pair of scarlet walls. And the details: monogrammed linen, superb Philippe Starck bathrooms in chrome and ground glass. It feels really good and the bar still attracts a few glitterati in the evenings.

Rooms: 32, including 3 junior suites.
Price: Singles & doubles 1000-1600 Frs (€152.45-243.92); junior suites 1800-2500 Frs.
Breakfast: 80 Frs.
Meals: On request 100-200 Frs.
Metro: St Germain des Prés.
RER: St Michel-Notre Dame.
Bus routes: 39 48 63 86 95
Car park: St Germain des Prés.

On the outside, Rue Jacob is nothing but hotels, fabric designers and antique merchants. But push a solid oak door or two and you may find a hidden garden and the gift of peace.

Map No: 2 & 4   Entry No: 48

small
30 Frs

Hôtel du Danube

58 rue Jacob
75006 Paris

Tel: (0)1 42 60 34 70
Fax: (0)1 42 60 81 18
E-mail: info@hoteldanube.fr
Web: www.hoteldanube.fr

Monsieur Ferrand & Monsieur Sario

Built as a private mansion at the height of the Third Empire, this soft civilised hotel rejoices in a dazzling black and red *salon* (fascinating black-framed cane sofa) and a large, white patio where potted palms sit in summer, cast-iron garden tables can be laid for breakfast and elegant façades rise skywards. The quietest rooms look this way. Others have more activity — and more noise — under their double-glazed windows (the higher, the quieter). Style and comfort vary widely, twisty corridors change levels, it's a warm, long-lived-in place. Superb superior rooms have two windows, some very desirable antiques, armchairs and thick, smart fabrics, yet they feel intimate and friendly. Their bathrooms are carefully done too. Standard rooms all have the same blue-laminate bamboo-trim desk units and nice 'wooden-plank' wallpaper with some quaintly old-style bathroom tiling — but all necessities are there, of course; the attic Standard room is in fact the most appealing of these. And everyone meets in the delicious countrified breakfast room and appreciates the bevy of young, helpful staff at reception. I liked it a lot. *Internet access on ground floor.*

Rooms: 40.
Price: Singles & doubles 650-980 Frs (€99.09-149.4); suites 1250-1300 Frs.
Breakfast: 55 Frs.
Meals: No.
Metro: St Germain des Prés.
RER: Musée d'Orsay.
Bus routes: 39 48 63 95 96
Car park: St Germain des Prés.

Surprising that so glorious a figure as Napoleon should have such a small street for his surname — maybe they couldn't quite forget the 2 million who died fighting his battles.

Entry No: 49

Map No: 4

 50 Frs

Le Madison

143 boulevard Saint-Germain
75006 Paris

Tel: (0)1 40 51 60 00
Fax: (0)1 40 51 60 01
E-mail: resa@hotel-madison.com
Web: www.hotel-madison.com

Maryse Burkard

Set back from the boulevard's jostle behind a row of trees, opposite the vastly celebrated *Deux Magots* café, the Madison's distinguished Art Deco façade is as supremely Parisian as its antique-filled *salons*. The enlightened owner likes sharing his collection and a fine portrait of his mother as a young girl dominates the breakfast area while a powerful porcelain cockerel crows on a china pedestal. This is a very stylish city hotel with fabrics and fittings of the highest quality yet it's never boring: Maryse Burkard's adventurous imagination guides the rich choice of colours and textures, bathrooms have stunning Italian tiling and staff have just the right mix of class and 1990s cheerfulness. All rooms are different, bursting with personality. One of the larger, two-windowed rooms over the boulevard in blue, beige and green has a fine dark green china lamp on a nice old desk and a deep red marble bathroom. Next door is a small room that clients love or loathe — deep raspberry, bright yellow, royal blue... vital and provocative! Lastly, the top-floor suite (illustrated) is a triumph of space and wraparound views of Paris. If the Madison is full, try the Bourgogne & Montana.

Rooms: 54.
Price: Singles & doubles 850-1700 Frs (€129.58-259.16); suite 1700-2500 Frs.
Breakfast: Included.
Meals: On request 100-150 Frs.
Metro: St Germain des Prés.
RER: Châtelet-Les Halles.
Bus routes: 48 58 63 70 86 87 95 96
Car park: St Germain des Prés.

In an earlier life, the Madison was a simple place of rest for thin purses: Camus stayed here when writing *L'Etranger*. Now big-name fashion boutiques draw the fatter wallets.

Hôtel de l'Académie

32 rue des Saints Pères
75007 Paris

Gérard Chekroun

Tel: (0)1 45 49 80 00
Toll-free USA 1 800 246 0041
Fax: (0)1 45 49 80 10
E-mail: academiehotel@aol.com
Web: www.academiehotel.com

When you push the door into this white building, you leave a street bustling with motor traffic and beautiful people for a quiet haven. Relaxed staff welcome you to the old-fashioned atmosphere of a *salon* furnished in Napoleon III style: gildings and furbelows, tassels and cup-bearing damsels beneath a glass canopy. With contemporary expectations in mind, bathrooms are fully equipped, bedding is new. I found the plain-painted walls a restful way of setting off the old beams and choice pieces such as a nice old ormulu Louis XV chest with its elaborate bronze fittings. A couple of little kidney-shaped bedside tables were a delight. The ground-floor breakfast room is cleverly arranged, playing with mirrors and infinite depths — the two round tables set between two mirrors and seductively close to the Juno figure are said to be very popular. You can have a caterer dinner here too if you wish. Bedrooms are biggish, by Paris standards, and storage space has been carefully planned. And, to cap it all, Monsieur Chekroun offers our readers a free bottle of red (Haut Médoc or Saint Émilion) or white (Sancerre or Chablis) wine... so take this book with you.

Rooms: 35, including 5 suites with whirlpool bath.
Price: Singles & doubles 490-1290 Frs (€74.70-196.66); suites 990-2580 Frs.
Breakfast: Full buffet 75 Frs.
Meals: On request about 150 Frs.
Metro: St Germain des Prés.
RER: Musée d'Orsay.
Bus routes: 48 63 86 95
Car park: Nearby: ask hotel.

The 'Saint Fathers' in question were not monks of the Abbey of St Germain: the name is a deformation of St Pierre, an old parish church now the Ukrainian Catholic church of St Vladimir.

Entry No: 51   Map No: 2 & 4

Hôtel Lenox Saint Germain

9 rue de l'Université
75007 Paris

Tel: (0)1 42 96 10 95
Fax: (0)1 42 61 52 83
E-mail: hotel@lenoxsaintgermain.com
Web: www.lenoxsaintgermain.com

Madame Laporte & Mademoiselle Colson

The wonderful jazzmen-inlaid Lenox Club bar has tremendous atmosphere. It is used by publishers for drinks after work, by film stars for interviews, by writers for long literary arguments — utterly St Germain des Prés and great fun, but no longer the breakfast room (in the vaulted basement now). The hotel entrance and lobby have been transformed into a serious symphony of pure 1930s style: strict lines, plain natural materials, a fascinating frieze motif and another superb framed inlay of a panther. Some great bronze animals too. Staff are friendly and will make you feel immediately welcome. Upstairs, there are large rooms and (much) smaller ones, all different. Some have old furniture, some have more modern and synthetic units, there are hand-painted cupboards and intriguing 1930s pieces; colours are mostly muted; rooms on the little Rue du Pré aux Clercs are quieter than the others; you may have the added luxury of a balcony. We really liked the corner rooms with two windows and lots of light. Bathrooms are good and extra shelving for pots and paints is provided by little trolleys. An excellent place to make you feel you belong in St Germain.

Rooms: 34.
Price: Singles, doubles, suites 720-1700 Frs (€109.76-259.16).
Breakfast: Continental 55 Frs; buffet 75 Frs.
Meals: Lenox Club snacks 35-100 Frs.
Metro: St Germain des Prés.
RER: Musée d'Orsay.
Bus routes: 48 39 63 68 69 83 94
Car park: Rue des Saints Pères.

The tramp hero of *Les Amants du Pont Neuf* spent a month in the Best Room here while filming but was forbidden to wash for the sake of more authentic tramphood. He had his own sheets.

Map No: 4 **Entry No: 52**

Hôtel de l'Université

22 rue de l'Université
75007 Paris

Tel: (0)1 42 61 09 39
Fax: (0)1 42 60 40 84
E-mail: hoteluniversite@gofornet.com
Web: www.hoteluniversite.com

Madame Bergmann & Monsieur Teissedre

In a city where a square metre is worth a small fortune, the double-doored entrance, the vista through to the green patio, the split-level, timber-framed sitting room, the wide staircase leading to high-ceilinged bedrooms are a privilege — even the smaller rooms are pretty, with neat little bathrooms. It is decorated like a grand embracing home with antiques and *objets* that Madame Bergmann has discovered far and wide over the years: tapestries in the right places, old prints in old frames ("Authentic or nothing — I don't hold with copies" she says), carvings, lamps. The breakfast room gives onto the tiny patio: you eat at a long bistro table on a long black velvet bench (or under the honeysuckle if you have taken one of the stunning terrace rooms). Most rooms have writing table or armchair or sofa and peaceful colours to set them off, some have the original panelling and built-in cupboards. Bathrooms are good — lots of marble and the right accessories — and so are views — neo-classical ministry portico, the École Nationale d'Administration, academic cradle of many a great career. The Université is a determinedly old-fashioned and eminently civilised delight for the discerning.

Rooms: 27, including 2 with terrace.
Price: Singles & doubles 800-1300 Frs
(€121.96-198.18).
Breakfast: Continental plus 50 Frs.
Meals: Light meals 50-150 Frs.
Metro: St Germain des Prés.
RER: Musée d'Orsay.
Bus routes: 24 27 39 48 63 68 69 70
87 95
Car park: Montalembert.

In the 12th century, the monks of St Germain Abbey used to have their ice house in the powerfully vaulted basement of this hotel, where there is now a superb meeting room for guests.

Entry No: 53

Map No: 2 & 4

Hôtel Verneuil

8 rue de Verneuil
75007 Paris

Tel: (0)1 42 60 82 14
Fax: (0)1 42 61 40 38
E-mail: verneuil@cybercable.fr
Web: www.france-hotel-guide.com/h75007verneuil.htm

Sylvie de Lattre

Sylvie de Lattre's intention is to make her guests feel as at home as in a private house; she has achieved her aim, brilliantly, and has such a natural sense of welcome that you are instantly at ease. The warm *salon* is like a country drawing room furnished with variegated pieces of family history, tempting books, chairs to curl up in; the smallish bedrooms (some only just make three-star size), all different, have painted beams or carved bedheads or a canopied bed or neo-classical pilasters. There is a fascinating variety of engravings, portraits and drawings, chosen room by room. The décor is one of understated strength, bedcovers are thick white piqué, walls are dressed in fine fabrics or plain pastels to set off other features. Firm-mattressed beds are high enough for suitcases to hide under and windows are hung with fine linen nets as well as beautiful co-ordinated curtains. One 'regular' room is like a little red box, warm and intimate, reached by walking under a massive old beam. Bathrooms are small but complete and the vaulted basement breakfast room has an easy rustic air. Quietly classy, this is a delicious find among the St Germain antique shops.

Rooms: 26.
Price: Singles & doubles 720-1100 Frs (€109.76-167.69).
Breakfast: Continental buffet 60 Frs.
Meals: On request 150 Frs.
Metro: St Germain des Prés, Rue du Bac.
RER: Musée d'Orsay, St Michel-Notre Dame.
Bus routes: 39 48 68 69 73 95
Car park: St Germain des Prés.

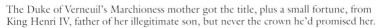

The Duke of Verneuil's Marchioness mother got the title, plus a small fortune, from King Henri IV, father of her illegitimate son, but never the crown he'd promised her.

Map No: 2 & 4   **Entry No: 54**

Hôtel de Lille

40 rue de Lille
75007 Paris

Tel: (0)1 42 61 29 09
Fax: (0)1 42 61 53 97
E-mail: hotel-de-lille@wanadoo.fr

Michel Margouilla

Between the cafés of St Germain des Prés, where the fun-loving crowd congregates, and the intense culture trip of the Orsay Museum, this small, clean-cut, impeccable hotel is a bargain among the smart antique shops. The strict 1930s style of the lobby is softened by big packets of greenery by the window. And when you go down to breakfast, you enter another universe. The vast stone vaults feel ancient indeed and garden-style soft-padded wicker furniture makes it a tempting space. Bedrooms are to scale: compact, furnished either with a 1930s veneered cupboard or desk or with cane-and-bamboo pieces; white walls and red carpets are a good foil to lively co-ordinated prints of curtain, quilt and stools; top-floor rooms are even cosier with their beams. One room is all done in the same print of a collection of Chinamen at a hot-air balloon launch — a humorous touch. Bathrooms are amazingly good for 20 years old! Marie-José, the delightful receptionist, and the owner himself are friendly and relaxed, but he keeps an eagle eye on the state of your quilt and the bathroom tiles. Refurbishment is constant, hair dryers are in place, the bar is most attractive.

Rooms: 20.
Price: Singles & doubles 560-850 Frs (€85.37-129.58), including breakfast.
Breakfast: Included.
Meals: No.
Metro: Rue du Bac, St Germain des Prés, Tuileries.
RER: Musée d'Orsay.
Bus routes: 48 49 68 69 95
Car park: Montalembert.

You may remember the Lille from your student days when washing facilities were communal, the price was 30F per night and the walls were made of cork!

Entry No: 55

Map No: 2 & 4

Hôtel du Quai Voltaire

19 quai Voltaire
75007 Paris

Tel: (0)1 42 61 50 91
Fax: (0)1 42 61 62 26
E-mail: info@hotelduquaivoltaire.com
Web: www.hotelduquaivoltaire.com

Régine Lepeinteur

Oscar Wilde once declared that he "never looked out of the window" — unthinkable when you stay here, where only four rooms do not see the Pissarro painting of quintessential Paris through their windows. Baudelaire also stayed here, as did Wagner and Sibelius: the Voltaire was something of a 'literary' institution and still feels like a well-loved club with its rather worn golden-fringed armchairs in the pannelled *salon* and its guests who come back again and again, some for over 30 years (I met one there). Rooms are small, beds are the standard French 1m40 width, some baths are not for reclining, but mattresses are good, staff are superb old retainers and the welcoming atmosphere is warmly genuine. The new manageress is lively, humorous and enthusiastic and plans to brighten the corridors with some fresh paint and change curtain fabrics, all the better to frame that ineffable view. New bathroom fixtures will follow. She loves the contact with guests, old and new. However, take earplugs: the price of that view is limited protection (double glazing only) against riverside traffic noise. *There are three top-floor singles with a bathroom on the floor below at bargain prices.*

Rooms: 33, including 3 triples.
Price: Singles & doubles 600-750 Frs (€91.47-114.34); triples 900 Frs.
Breakfast: 50 Frs.
Meals: No.
Metro: Rue du Bac, Tuileries.
RER: Musée d'Orsay.
Bus routes: 24 27 39 48 68 73 95
Car park: Musée d'Orsay.

One of Pissarro's paintings — his magic vision of the Seine, the Pont Royal, the Louvre and the trees along the embankment — can be seen at Orsay just down the road; the others are in Russia...

Map No: 2 & 4

Entry No: 56

Hôtel d'Orsay

93 rue de Lille
75007 Paris

Tel: (0)1 47 05 85 54
Fax: (0)1 45 55 51 16
E-mail: hotel.orsay@wanadoo.fr
Web: www.esprit-de-france.com

David Chevalier

This is the story of a resurrection: two run-down hotels with very beautiful façades, the Solferino and the Orsay, have been thrown together and deeply converted for 21st-century comfort (the attention to detail and design goes as far as smooth, bi-coloured wood light switches). The great lobby flows into the sitting area on a vast expanse of finely-striped rich-beige carpet studded with raspberry-plush bucket chairs. Luscious antiques sit here and there and a great pane of glass at the back is filled with the greenery of a small cleverly-sloped indoor garden. Rooms vary in style, some are prettily floral and feminine, others are more soberly businesslike, all have antique desks and bedside tables. Gently lovely colours — ginger and yellow, salmon pink and beige, red and soft green — clothe beds and windows; new bathrooms are tiled and mirrored to a T. The best rooms are, naturally, the suites but even the smallest is sweetly hidden up a little staircase. Some rooms and the future breakfast room (a big space beneath a pair of huge roof windows) are still being renovated. Orsay Museum is just steps away, the Louvre is reached in five minutes over the new footbridge. A super place to stay.

Rooms: 41.
Price: Singles & doubles 600-850 Frs (€91.47-129.58); suites 1350-1500 Frs.
Breakfast: 50 Frs.
Meals: On request 100-200 Frs.
Metro: Solférino.
RER: Musée d'Orsay.
Bus routes: 63 73 84 94
Car park: Montalembert.

It was after the battle of Solférino in 1859 that Swissman Henri Dunant, deeply disturbed by the sight of so many wounded yet untreated soldiers, founded the Red Cross.

Entry No: 57   Map No: 2 & 4

 80 Frs

Hôtel Bourgogne et Montana

3 rue de Bourgogne
75007 Paris

Tel: (0)1 45 51 20 22
Fax: (0)1 45 56 11 98
Web: www.bourgogne-montana.com

Stéphane Beauvivre

Important people (MPs) dash about these streets behind the National Assembly and it is a delicious relief to enter the peaceful Bourgogne where the lift is a wonder of pre-war oak and ironwork and you find a combination of efficiency and wit — the French at their best. The staff know how to marry serious attention to guests and a light-hearted welcome; the owner's grandfather, a bored MP in the 1890s, drew those wicked caricatures of his solemn colleagues; his own antiques and pictures grace the famous rotunda with its dark pink pilasters and bar, the *salon* with its leather chairs and the deeply tempting breakfast room that is full of light and the most sinful buffet (included in the price). It IS a luxy hotel, worth its four stars, so abandon yourself to the caress of fine damasks, deep velvet and Frencher-than-French Jouy. The bigger rooms have space and antiques, lovely china lamps, thick quilted upholstery and some extraordinary bathrooms; the smaller ones are like rich, embracing nests. The big apartment, supremely stylish in white, grey and pale yellow, has two bathrooms and a huge draped bed. And there's that feast for breakfast. If the hotel is full, try the Madison.

Rooms: 32.
Price: Singles & doubles 900-1350 Frs (€137.20-205.81); suites 1850-2200 Frs.
Breakfast: Buffet included.
Meals: No.
Metro: Assemblée Nationale, Invalides.
RER & Air France bus: Invalides.
Bus routes: 93 83 63
Car park: Invalides.

This Duke of Burgundy (Bourgogne), father of Louis XV, once famously told his Sun King of a grandfather, Louis XIV : "A king is made for his subjects, not subjects for their king".

Map No: 1 & 3

Entry No: 58

Le Service

Invalides – Eiffel Tower

Hôtel de Varenne
44 rue de Bourgogne
75007 Paris

Tel: (0)1 45 51 45 55
Fax: (0)1 45 51 86 63
E-mail: hotel.varenne@wanadoo.fr

Maurice Janin

 30 Frs

That garden courtyard, alive with *Impatiens* and eager ivies, is a blessed surprise as you come in from the city street where men in suits dash up and down. You feel you are walking up to a country house (all but four of the bedrooms look over courtyards); in summer, there are cast-iron conservatory tables out here for quiet breakfasts, too. Inside, you soon recognise that the house colour is a soft *Vieux Rose*. The smart breakfast room has green chairs in contrast and two big somewhat surrealistic pictures of people doing smart city things on beaches: a spot of humour that makes it all very human and civilised. The country house atmosphere extends to the bedrooms, where there is a lot of soft deep pink or beige on walls and floors, plus greens and creams and coffee colours in curtains and friezes. No two rooms are alike, most are a reasonable size, and all have one or two really nice old pieces of furniture; there are plush-covered bucket armchairs, attractive framed prints and well-kept bathrooms. But the priority here is service. The charming staff are constantly on the lookout for more they can do to make your stay really special.

Rooms: 24.
Price: Singles & doubles 660-780 Frs (€100.62-118.91).
Breakfast: 56 Frs.
Meals: No.
Metro: Varenne, Invalides.
RER: Invalides.
Bus routes: 69
Car park: Invalides.

In old French, *varenne* meant uncultivated, game-rich land. In the 16th century, this area of 'Paris' was a royal reserve and the King would ride out from the Louvre to hunt here.

Entry No: 59   Map No: 1 & 3

Hôtel du Palais Bourbon
49 rue de Bourgogne
75007 Paris

Tel: (0)1 44 11 30 70
Fax: (0)1 45 55 20 21
E-mail: htlbourbon@aol.com
Web: www.hotel-palais-bourbon.com

Thierry Claudon

In a district of fine old mansions — now occupied by civil servants, of course — nothing prepares you for the hotel that spreads and rambles here: don't miss the discreet doorway. You will be greeted by the delightful South American Rafael, or Monsieur Claudon, or Madame Mère — the atmosphere is comfortably casual and loyal staff stay for years. After the fresh, high-beamed breakfast room and lobby, you enter the depths and discover something resembling a simple, quiet, country house in two connecting buildings full of secret spaces. Gently unsteep staircases announce their 18th-century origins; all the rooms are different, those on the lower floors are unusually big for two Parisian stars, top-floor doubles have beamy character and the little singles are excellent value. Décor is quiet and unprovocative: soft pastels in peachy paint, mild stripes, delicate florals. Each room has an individual touch, be it an oriental rug or a country antique, and essential furniture — beds, wardrobes, desk units — is custom-made in Brittany. Bathrooms, recently renovated, are simply excellent with white tiling and pretty friezes, ultra-modern tap fittings, generous space. Altogether excellent value.

Rooms: 32, including 4 singles sharing shower & wc.
Price: Singles & doubles 300-670 Frs (€45.73-102.14), triples 770 Frs, quadruples 850 Frs.
Breakfast: Included.
Meals: No.
Metro: Invalides, Varenne, Assemblée Nationale. **RER:** Invalides.
Bus routes: 24 63 69 73 83 84 94
Car park: Invalides.

The 'Bourbon Palace' was seized from its aristocratic owners in 1790 to become the 'House of the Revolution' and has housed the National Assembly since the Restoration.

Map No: 1 & 3

Entry No: 60

Hôtel Bailli de Suffren – Tour Eiffel

149 avenue de Suffren   **Tel:** (0)1 56 58 64 64
75015 Paris   **Fax:** (0)1 45 67 75 82
                    E-mail: bailli.suffren.hotel@wanadoo.fr
                    Web: www.123france.com/bailli-de-suffren

Monsieur & Madame Tardif

An unreservedly French and supremely welcoming hotel. The smart city *salon* that greets you says it all, in ormolu, gilt and swags (illustrated but soon to be 'updated'... from 18th to 19-century style). Beyond it you discover the deliciously countrified dining room where pink and mirrored walls and pretty curly chairs call you to buffet breakfast, or refined supper with wine from Provençal vineyards once owned by the Marquis de Suffren. At 7pm, wines and *Kir* are served in the lounge and there's a permanent exhibition of excellent paintings by Brigitte du Mérac (for sale, like the wine). Bedrooms, giving onto warm corridors where oriental rugs and old marine prints remind you of the Bailiff's travels, are smallish, soft and attractive but not fussy, in co-ordinated colours with neat bathrooms. The *Chambre du Bailli* is more marine-minded than the others with richly-striped fabrics and a wonderful wood-panelled, porthole-mirrored captain's shower room. The Tardifs, relaxed and knowledgeable, run a highly civilised establishment that is a credit to French tradition and much loved by the great and the good who frequent the halls of UNESCO nearby.

Rooms: 25.
Price: Singles & doubles 695-950 Frs (€105.95-144.83); apartments 1495-1595 Frs.
Breakfast: In room 50 Frs; buffet 70 Frs.
Meals: Hotel menu 95 Frs (& à la carte).
Metro: Ségur, Sèvres-Lecourbe.
RER: Champ de Mars.
Bus routes: 39 70 89
Car park: Consult hotel.

This 18th-century Bailiff was a superior of the Order of the Cross of Malta and a swashbuckling Admiral, not the nasty arm of the law collecting TV sets to pay the taxman.

Entry No: 61   Map No: 3

Hôtel Le Tourville

16 avenue de Tourville
75007 Paris

Tel: (0)1 47 05 62 62
Fax: (0)1 47 05 43 90
E-mail: hotel@tourville.com
Web: www.hoteltourville.com

Michel Bouvier & Thierry Jacquet

On a calm avenue near the Champ de Mars, a good-value four-star hotel where the attentive welcome you receive is worth a skyful of stars. A soft, cushioned impression flows from deep carpets with Turkey rugs (rugs lighten and colour the whole hotel), plush sofas, indoor shutters to filter the afternoon sun, muted Vivaldi. Sensuous colours and shapes abound, soft strokable materials, gatepost ornaments on an Empire console: ironical decorative touches, full of intelligence and fun. Each room has a few 'finds' — a brass-handled chest, a Regency writing table, an old mirror, and more irony in frames. With the big ground-floor triple come a terrace and a fascinating neo-classical group of nude women; junior suites are generous with space, light — and more kitschy pictures. Colours are peach, salmon or frankly pink; some rooms are small for the category but all have good storage and super bathrooms (thick fluffy towels, marble finish), with maybe a Victorian clothes horse or an old nursery chair in contrast. Offsetting this simple sophistication, the vaulted breakfast room has a rustic air with its coconut matting, cane chairs and rough peachy walls.

Rooms: 30, including 3 junior suites.
Price: Singles, doubles, suites 890-1990 Frs (€135.68-303.37).
Breakfast: Continental plus 70 Frs.
Meals: On request 100-300 Frs.
Metro: Ecole Militaire. RER & Air France bus: Invalides.
Bus routes: 29 48 80 82 87 92
Car park: École Militaire.

Tourville was a romantic admiral called Anne (sic) who fought pirates in the Mediterranean and spent the 1690s locked in endless naval battles with the English in the Channel.

Map No: 3

Eiffel Park Hôtel

17 bis rue Amélie
75007 Paris

Tel: (0)1 45 55 10 01
Fax: (0)1 47 05 28 68
E-mail: eiffelpk@club-internet.fr
Web: www.france-hotel-guide.com/h75007eiffelpark.ht

Françoise Testard

Such transformation: the Eiffel Park started as a clean-cut, shiny business hotel — and had a change of heart involving lots of Asian furniture and *objets*. The granite floor of the high yellow hall is warmed with a big oriental rug, rattan colonial armchairs, a wonderful table made from a pair of Indian shutters and a gigantic Provençal urn. Pass a carved Indian gate to the soft-smart bar and *salon* then to the warmly Mediterranean Garcia-designed breakfast room and the little patio. All very comforting. Most rooms have some rustic-looking Far-Eastern furniture — little chests, bedside tables, often painted to match the colour scheme, which may be blue and sunny gold or vibrant pink and red, some in Jouy prints. Rooms are not big but there are some quirky shapes and window angles which give space; bathrooms have superb classic white tiles and fittings. The crowning glory is a wonderful summer roof terrace where grapes grow, lavender flowers and you can breakfast while gazing across the roofscape. A lively, friendly welcome completes the picture. *Four connecting apartments possible. ASP readers who stay three nights get their third breakfast free!*

Rooms: 36.
Price: Singles & doubles 1000-1200 Frs (€152.45-182.94).
Breakfast: Continental buffet 55 Frs. Free your third morning.
Meals: No.
Metro: La Tour Maubourg. RER & Air France bus: Invalides.
Bus routes: 28 49 63 69
Car park: Invalides.

Amélie Pihan de Laforêt died young and her father, who owned the land this street is built on, immortalised her name rather than his own: she was said to possess all the Christian virtues, aged 15.

Entry No: 63

Map No: 1 & 3

Grand Hôtel Lévêque

29 rue Cler
75007 Paris

Tel: (0)1 47 05 49 15
Fax: (0)1 45 50 49 36
E-mail: info@hotelleveque.com
Web: www.hotel-leveque.com

Christian Tourneur

There's so much to look at in this lively, colourful pedestrian street where the shops overflow onto the pavement that, were it not for the flags flying overhead, you might miss the door to the ever-popular Lévêque. At the end of the long classic-style hallway is the desk where the kindly, if occasionally busy, receptionist deals patiently with all comers: the constant flow of young international travellers makes for an amicable polyglot environment. The little semicircular sitting 'kiosk' with its red plush bench draws the eye: you may prefer to sit with the Parisians on the street, but do admire Alexandra de Lazareff's fascinating bronze animals before going out. They are proof, in a way, that the new owners respect their guests and want to create a civilised environment in this big, bustling house. In the breakfast room, the sepia mural of Notre Dame is another example of this attitude. More practically, there are fans for comfort and safes for reassurance in all rooms. Décor? Pretty much the same throughout, with 1930s-style laminated bedheads, green carpets, pastel fabrics and sometimes an old mirror-fronted wardrobe — all neat and clean with decent shower rooms and good beds.

Rooms: 50.
Price: Doubles & triples 400-600 Frs (€60.98-91.47).
Breakfast: 40 Frs.
Meals: No.
Metro: Ecole Militaire, Latour Maubourg. RER & Air France bus: Invalides.
Bus routes: 28 69 82 92
Car park: Latour Maubourg.

This area used to be Grenelle: a vast plain belonging to a great abbey with just a farm, a small château and a military execution block until the 1830s, when the developers moved in.

Map No: 1 & 3   **Entry No: 64**

Hôtel Relais Bosquet-Tour Eiffel

19 rue du Champ de Mars
75007 Paris

Tel: (0)1 47 05 25 45
Fax: (0)1 45 55 08 24
E-mail: hotel@relaisbosquet.com
Web: www.relaisbosquet.com

Dora & Philippe Hervois

Unexpectedly, beyond the unprepossessing doorway lies a colourful, cushioned *salon* and two attractive breakfast rooms (one for smokers). Then a long, Persian-rugged vista past twin patios where magnolia and creepers flourish. Half the rooms are round this courtyard, half look onto the street. The sense of space and peace comes with a remarkable sense of service: the people at reception, owners or staff, are quietly attentive; each room has iron and ironing board, kettle, four pillows, modem socket, masses of hangers and electrically-operated blackout blinds. The smart contemporary/traditional décor, either red, blue or green themed, avoids plushiness by its easy use of rich, bright, coordinated fabrics; big upholstered stools make superb suitcase racks; fine white bathrooms have just a sober colour trim. There's space in these rooms and good storage, beds are zippable twins (extra long in 'Superiors'), the lighting is just right. Every print has been chosen for its character, the occasional antique is an added personal touch and staff will organise baby-sitters or secretarial workers for you. A most likeable hotel two minutes from the Eiffel Tower.

Rooms: 40.
Price: Doubles 950-1150 Frs
(€144.83-175.32).
Breakfast: Generous Continental 65 Frs.
Meals: No.
Metro: Ecole Militaire.
RER: Pont de l'Alma.
Bus routes: 28 49 82 80 92
Car park: Hotel arranges.

General Bosquet saved the English army fighting under Lord Cardigan at Inkerman (Crimea) and was made Field Marshal AND Senator for it on his return to France in 1856.

Entry No: 65

Map No: 1 & 3

Hôtel de Londres Eiffel

1 rue Augereau
75007 Paris

Tel: (0)1 45 51 63 02
Fax: (0)1 47 05 28 96
E-mail: londres@club-internet.fr
Web: www.londres-eiffel.com

Isabelle Prigent

On a quiet little street half way between the Eiffel Tower (affectionately known as *La Grande Dame*) and the gilded lid over Napoleon's resting place (he was less kindly known as *Le Petit Caporal*), here is a friendly, warm-coloured hotel in butter yellow and raspberry pink, friezes and quilting. The mixture of fine blinds and heavy curtains makes for a most welcoming atmosphere in the lobby, which flows round into the sitting/dining area. Here, there are marble-topped tables, pink-skirted and beribboned chairs and gilt-framed mirrors. Beyond, past a pair of plant-filled lightwells, is the *Pavillon* with six bedrooms on two floors in sweet seclusion. All rooms play variations on the same pink and yellow theme with very pretty florals, checks and stripes — even the blankets under the bedcovers are co-ordinated ochre or red. The pale wood furniture is in old French style, there is even the odd country armoire. Bath and shower rooms are good, if a little more old-fashioned on the street side, with all useful equipment. But above all, you will be very well looked after by the eager and enthusiastic Madame Prigent.

Rooms: 30.
Price: Single, double, triple 565-815 Frs (€86.13-124.25).
Breakfast: Continental plus 40 Frs.
Meals: No.
Metro: École Militaire.
RER: Pont de l'Alma.
Bus routes: 69 80 87
Car park: École Militaire.

Augereau, humble son of a man-servant and a fruit-picker, rose to fame, glory and a whole rope of titles under Napoleon: Field Marshal, Duke and Great Eagle of the Legion of Honour.

Map No: 1 & 3

Entry No: 66

Hôtel de la Tulipe
33 rue Malar
75007 Paris

Tel: (0)1 45 51 67 21
Fax: (0)1 47 53 96 37
Web: www.hoteldelatulipe.com

Caroline &
Jean-Louis Fortuit

 80 Frs

The Tulipe, in its Provençal paints and prints, is as delightful as ever; your hosts are friendly, intelligent and a pleasure to meet. This has been an hotel since the influx of visitors to the *Exposition Universelle* in 1900 but it was once a convent. Deliciously intimate rooms are in the former nuns' cells (at least two cells per room!) on two storeys round the honeysuckled, cobbled courtyard or over the quiet street. Beams and old stones, yellow-sponged walls and deep red carpets, simple pine or wicker furniture, patchwork bedcovers or bright Provençal prints: the sun shines here every day of the year. Bathrooms have blue or yellow country-style tiling and bright butter-yellow paint. The two rooms that lead directly off the patio, one equipped for disabled guests, have a specially peaceful and connected feel because of this. The breakfast room is utterly charming with its pale stones, blond timbers, and interesting paintings... and croissants fresh from the local bakery. Above all, together with the unpretentious good taste of the Fortuit family we remember their smiles and relaxed manner and so, most certainly, will you.

Rooms: 21, including 1 family suite with 1 bathrooms.
Price: Singles & doubles 600-700 Frs (€91.47-106.71); triple 900 Frs; suite 1300 Frs.
Breakfast: Continental plus 50 Frs.
Meals: No.
Metro & RER: Invalides, Pont de l'Alma.
Bus routes: 49 63 69 80 92
Car park: Rue Malar.

The 7th arrondissement has some stupendous Art Nouveau buildings, many by Jules Lavirotte, a brilliant designer of cement fantasmagorias. Try Avenue Rapp for a taste.

Entry No: 67   Map No: 1

Passy – Trocadéro

 30 F

Hôtel Boileau

81 rue Boileau
75016 Paris

Tel: (0)1 42 88 83 74
Fax: (01) 45 27 62 98
E-mail: boileau@cybercable.fr
Web: www.hotel-boileau.com

Monsieur & Madame Guirec Mahé

Way out west, ideally placed for tennis at Roland Garros, football at the Parc des Princes and family outings to the Bois de Boulogne, the Boileau is a house of peace and memory whose sweet little face is decorated with bright blue gold-lettered awnings. Young, with an easy, welcoming manner, the Mahés have a collection of ancient sewing machines, cash registers and gramophones to delight lovers of early mechanical devices; mirrors, furniture and pictures from Brittany and Morocco to please the traveller; a fresh green patio, supervised by three dwarves, to bring light and air to the sitting and breakfast rooms at the centre of the three low buildings. Rooms are simply delightful, nothing posh, nothing superfluous, just good warm colour schemes, some original painted Breton bedheads, some lamps in Arab filigree work, interesting pictures and good, pretty bathrooms. Even the little singles have been given the personal touch. Oscar the parrot may talk to you at breakfast (a good spread), staff have been here for years, and they are all such nice people! Far out perhaps, but excellent value and a perfect spot for those coming from or going to Normandy or Brittany.

Rooms: 30.
Price: Single, double, triple 420-700 Frs (€64.03-106.71).
Breakfast: 40-45 Frs.
Meals: No.
Metro: Exelmans.
RER: Charles de Gaulle-Etoile.
Bus routes: 22 62 72 PC
Car park: Avenue de Versailles.

No 86 rue Boileau leads to Villa Mulhouse: 67 little houses built new and modern for his workers in 1835 by cotton magnate Dollfus who believed that "hygiene and morality go hand in hand".

Entry No: 68 Map No: 3

Hôtel Frémiet Eiffel

6 avenue Frémiet
75016 Paris

Tel: (0)1 45 24 52 06
Fax: (0)1 53 92 06 46
E-mail: hotel.fremiet@wanadoo.fr
Web: GDS: BestWesternNo93086

Madame Fourmond

The steep little street off Avenue Président Kennedy is a glorious piece of architectural symmetry dated 1913, all in curves and juttings, stone garlands and fantasies. The Frémiet has brilliantly kept the volumes and decorations of its first life as an apartment block and Monsieur Fourmond is proud to declare that guestrooms are NOT rational here but guests are most carefully attended to. From the lovely staircase (superb original windows), each landing has a grand double door into the original 10ft-high 160m² apartment, now divided up. The former drawing room, now a generous bedroom, has a curved window onto a balcony with view of the Seine; the former kitchen is a huge bathroom with double basin and a cockerel crowing in the tiling. Overall, it is a lesson in French apartment design just before society collapsed into the Great War. The degree of comfort matches the grand atmosphere: classic Louis XV and Louis XVI pieces, some built-in practicalities, contemporary colour schemes and the occasional touch by the owner's designer daughter; all rooms are fully soundproofed. The welcome is high-class, too — it's a wonderful place.

Rooms: 36, including 2 suites.
Price: Single, double, suite 600-2000 Frs (€91.47-304.90).
Breakfast: 70 Frs.
Meals: On request 100-200 Frs.
Metro: Passy.
RER: Champ de Mars.
Bus routes: 32 72
Car park: In street or garage 200m.

In the Wine Museum just up the road, deep galleries plunge into the hillside to take you through the history of French wine. Your ticket includes a tasting; you can even lunch there.

Map No: 1 & 3   **Entry No:** 69

Hôtel Gavarni
5 rue Gavarni
75116 Paris

Tel: (0)1 45 24 52 82
Fax: (0)1 40 50 16 95
E-mail: reservation@gavarni.com
Web: www.gavarni.com

Nelly Rolland

△
▽ 🐑 suites

Mademoiselle Rolland! Her welcome is as warm as her laugh is silvery and you will be captivated by her neat little hotel, all decked out in rich dark green and soft pale yellow, where the atmosphere is young and thoroughly unpompous. And from 2001, those who love Passy and the Gavarni will have an amazing choice: the small, snug, two-star rooms they already know or the new and beautiful suites their hostess is installing on the upper floors, in an atmosphere of "simple (air-conditioned) luxury". The ground floor is mirrored and arm-chaired to a T, the cosy breakfast area has little round tables and Bauhaus chairs — unfussy airiness pervades under the mural of a giant pot of flowers. The sponged paintwork, green carpet and pastel draperies are still fresh in their light splotchy floral curtains and quilts. Bathrooms, reached through space-saving folding doors, are not big but contain all the essentials, while hairdryers are mounted outside beside the full-length wall mirrors. In a quiet residential side street, a step away from smart shopping on Rue de Passy, a short walk from the Eiffel Tower or the Trocadéro with its museums and elegant cafés, the Gavarni is a delight.

Rooms: 25, including 5 suites.
Price: Singles & doubles 415-560 Frs (€63.27-85.37); suites 2000 Frs and over.
Breakfast: 38 Frs & à la carte.
Meals: On request 100-150 Frs.
Metro: Passy, Trocadéro.
RER: Boulainvilliers.
Bus routes: 22 32
Car park: Garage Moderne, Rue de Passy.

Proper names? The Basque satirical cartoonist Chevalier adopted the name *Gavarni* in honour of a Pyrenean geological cirque near Roland's Gap that he came to love.

Entry No: 70   Map No: 1 & 3

Le Hameau de Passy

48 rue de Passy
75016 Paris

Tel: (0)1 42 88 47 55
Fax: 90)1 42 30 83 72
E-mail: hameau.passy@wanadoo.fr

Madame Brepson

  40 Frs

The setting is such a surprise: yet another secret garden behind the shopping frenzy of Rue de Passy — through the archway and here is real shelter from traffic. It is all very long and thin, but there's room for a line of tall trees, lots of grass and flowering shrubs and tables outside in good weather. Along one side of the cul-de-sac, the hotel is made of two newer bits added to the old building, each with a modern fully-glazed version of the medieval stair tower (the lift serves half the rooms). The eager new owners are renovating in bits too. Some bathrooms are already pretty with new tiles and fittings, others, waiting for the treatment, are perfectly adequate but not so pretty; all will soon be finished. Bedrooms are decorated in soft/strong colours: coral pink, moss green, aquamarine or salmon. They vary in size but are very acceptable two-star rooms with furniture in colour-stained wood or bamboo and wicker and the odd brass bedhead; the atticky rooms are fun and some can be connected to form family apartments. Air and light and silence — bar the birdsong, of course. Hotel guests and apartment residents on the other side of the garden take great care to avoid disturbing each other.

Rooms: 32.
Price: Singles & doubles 450-630 Frs (€68.6-96.04), including breakfast.
Breakfast: Included.
Meals: No.
Metro: Passy, La Muette.
RER: Boulainvilliers.
Bus routes: 32
Car park: 19 rue de Passy (ask hotel).

In 1840, the great author Honoré de Balzac moved to a house near here to escape his creditors, only opening the door to those who knew his password "Plums are in season".

Map No: 1 & 3   **Entry No:** 71

Hôtel Nicolo

3 rue Nicolo
75016 Paris

Tel: (0)1 42 88 83 40
Fax: (0)1 42 24 45 41
E-mail: hotel.nicolo@wanadoo.fr

Catherine and her team

Such a surprise! A hidden entrance, beneath one building, across a courtyard of acacia and evergreen, into another. All is hushed, the old mosaic floor smiles at you, French Granny's sitting room opens up on your right, you are greeted by delightful staff who have known and loved the Nicolo for many years. And now new owners have brought new, many-splendoured furnishings, fabrics, pictures by artist friends (old engravings coloured 'in the manner of', pastels of Port Grimaud, a powerful parrot series). The renovated rooms are stunning, the others will do perfectly until they can join the élite, all give onto courtyards, of course. The new? Lovely lacey-carved Indonesian screens have become voluptuous three-arched bedheads with original paintwork, fabric panels, bird and animal figures. Desks and tables are unusual Dutch, French or oriental antiques; lamps are unusual modern objects. Pure white beds have quilts in broad, rich stripes. Here are richness and purity married, and the few new bathrooms are luscious. The old? 1970s beiges, some oriental florals, some red carpet — all comfortable and friendly, all due to go soon. A fascinating study in change and a super place to stay.

Rooms: 28, including 4 family rooms.
Price: Single, double, family rooms
440-770 Frs (€67.08-117.39).
Breakfast: 35 Frs.
Meals: No.
Metro: Passy, La Muette.
RER: Boulainvilliers.
Bus routes: 22 32
Car park: Consult hotel.

Nicolo was destined to be a Maltese merchant but became a Parisian composer of light operas that enchanted Napoleonic France. One of his best-loved works was *The Lottery Ticket*.

Entry No: 72   Map No: 1 & 3

Hôtel Massenet
5 bis rue Massenet
75116 Paris

Tel: (0)1 45 24 43 03
Fax: (0)1 45 24 41 39
E-mail: hotel.massenet@wanadoo.fr

Bernard Mathieu

For 70 years, the Mathieu family has cultivated the art of attentive welcome behind this balconied 1900s façade, and the fruit is a most welcoming, civilised place. The panelled and mirrored ground floor has the atmosphere of a quiet club with deep leather armchairs, a bar and interesting pictures framed by Madame Mathieu, who has a shop locally. The green and yellow breakfast room is a light fresh space that opens onto a much-planted little patio where you can sit in summer. Upstairs, rooms are classically muted: eggshell walls, dark green or deep ginger carpets, some adventurously bright bedcovers or curtains, one or two good pieces of old furniture, more interesting pictures on the walls, good storage and room to sit peacefully. One pair of singles is suddenly more feminine in satiny, musliny, peachy softness. At the top, two rooms have terraces whence you can survey miles of rooftops: lovely for breakfast or lounging. Some bathrooms have been more recently renovated, one is still in its super 1930s mosaic garb. All linen is bordered and monogrammed and all rooms except the smallest have double doors from the corridor. The feel is of deep quilted comfort and old-style class.

Rooms: 41.
Price: Singles & doubles 555-845 Frs
(€84.61-128.82).
Breakfast: 45 Frs.
Meals: On request 100-300 Frs.
Metro: La Muette, Passy.
RER: Boulainvilliers.
Bus routes: 22 32 52
Car park: 19 rue de Passy.

300 years ago, Passy was a country village where society ladies came for the fertility-enhancing waters; now it is part of gentrified Paris where they shop and entertain.

Map No: 1 & 3 Entry No: 73

Les Jardins du Trocadéro

35 rue Benjamin Franklin
75116 Paris

Tel: (0)1 53 70 17 70
Fax: (0)1 53 70 17 80
E-mail: jardintroc@aol.com
Web: www.jardintroc.com

Katia Chekroun

Intimate, relaxed, lavish and fun — a listed building with exuberantly Napoleon III décor, when the motto was "Too much is not enough". Behind the bronze-decorated door, two Egyptian torch-bearers salute; Muses beckon from landing walls; musical monkeys gambol across door panels (all painted by Beaux Arts students). The atmosphere is young and casual but efficiency and service are there, discreet and unobsequious. Lovers of the small and intimate will like it here; so will fans of French style. The gilt-mirrored, bronze-lamped *salon* has pure Second Empire furniture on a perfectly aged marble floor and drinks are served at a genuine custom-made bistro bar, *le zinc*. The great junior suite is magnificently regal in crimson and gold (plus matching telephone) with green touches and langorous neo-classical pictures. Otherwise, don't expect big rooms (the 'executive' rooms are larger and good suites can be organised) but enjoy their soft generous draperies and the genuine antiques (many ormolu-trimmed Boulle-type pieces) that the owners took such trouble finding then, surrounded by marble, luxuriate in your whirlpool bath and fluffy bathrobe.

Rooms: 18 with whirlpool bath.
Price: Singles & doubles 890-2600 Frs
(€135.68-396.37).
Breakfast: 'Unlimited' buffet 75 Frs.
Meals: On request 100-200 Frs.
Metro: Trocadéro.
RER: Charles de Gaulle-Etoile.
Bus routes: 22 30 32 63
Car park: Hotel.

Franklin's active opposition to England greatly endeared him to France and the French government declared three whole days of national mourning when he died in 1790.

Entry No: 74   Map No: 1

Grand Palais – Petit Palais

•

Haute couture

•

Place de la Concorde

•

La Madeleine church

Étoile – Champs Elysées

Hôtel Kléber

7 rue de Belloy
75116 Paris

Tel: (0)1 47 23 80 22
Fax: (0)1 49 52 07 20
E-mail: kleberhotel@aol.com
Web: www.kleberhotel.com

Samuel Abergel

A Napoleonic wind (Napoleon III, of course) has swept the Kléber's ground floor, opening up new vistas, depositing trompe-l'œil draperies and costumed monkeys on walls (including the artist herself, marching off with hat, palette and parrot), a splendid glass roof over the lovely aged-marble floor and unashamedly ornate, damasked furniture upon it. Stupendous — and saved from excess by fine, plain oak panelling. The family, who also own the Académie and the Jardins du Trocadéro, love hunting for period pieces for their hotels, hence the rococo lamps, encrustations, kitschy paintings and life-size statues. The suite has a beautiful inlaid roll-top desk in its balconied *salon*, and even a kitchenette. All the décor is rich in colour — reds, yellows, blues — and texture; tiled or mosaic bathrooms are not big but are well designed and some have whirlpool baths. Samy's warm welcome is confirmed by the basket of fruit and chocolates awaiting you in your room and the breakfast buffet includes home-made jams and croissants, cereals, cheese and eggs for a fine start to the day. A cosmopolitan atmosphere where English, Spanish, Hebrew, Japanese and Arabic are spoken.

Rooms: 22, including 1 suite.
Price: Singles & doubles 790-1590 Frs (€120.43-242.39).
Breakfast: Full buffet 75 Frs.
Meals: On request 100-200 Frs.
Metro: Kléber, Boissière.
RER: Charles de Gaulle-Étoile.
Bus routes: 22 30 82 63
Car park: Hotel.

Kléber, soldier son of an Alsatian pastry cook, couldn't, as a commoner, hope for officer rank in the King's army but rose fast after the Revolution killed the King: he died a General under Napoleon.

Entry No: 75

Map No: 1

 50 Frs

Hôtel Franklin Roosevelt

18 rue Clément Marot
75008 Paris

Tel: (0)1 53 57 49 50
Fax: (0)1 47 20 44 30
E-mail: franklin@iway.fr
Web: www.franklin-roosevelt.com

David Le Boudec

This is a 'sandwich' hoTel: the ground floor and two top floors have been lushly converted by the new owners into a very superior establishment: an 'English club lounge' below — mahogany bar, leather Chesterfields, thick carpets — and high-class suites and rooms off wide, silent corridors above. Up here there's more mahogany (even the bath panels), walls cloaked in moiré and thick silky curtains on big brass rods. Subtle, sober colour schemes have maximum designer power where the occasional inlaid cupboard or whirlpool bath, stripey-marble shower or Patrick Ireland engraving completes the sense of privilege. Most rooms on the middle floors, called 'Japanese' or 'Bamboo', have the luxury of size and are perfectly comfortable but simpler and cheaper: 'normal'-size beds, plain walls (apart from some wonderful murals – a Mississippi panorama room, several trompe-l'œil pictures) and good bathrooms. But guests from all floors naturally bathe in the intimate pine-panelled sitting room, the pretty rattan-furnished breakfast room and the brilliantly canopied winter garden. Your young host is attentive and enthusiastic and you should feel well looked after.

Rooms: 48.
Price: Doubles/twins 945-2200 Frs (€144.06-335.39); suites 2200-3500 Frs.
Breakfast: Continental 75 Frs; generous buffet 120 Frs.
Meals: No.
Metro: Franklin Roosevelt.
RER: Charles de Gaulle-Étoile.
Bus routes: 32 42 80
Car park: Rue Marbeuf.

At 49 rue Pierre Charron is Pershing Hall with an American Legion emblem carved over an elaborate gate and 3 window keystones depicting US sailor, soldier, airman.

 small

Hôtel de l'Élysée

12 rue des Saussaies
75008 Paris

Tel: (0)1 42 65 29 25
Fax: (0)1 42 65 64 28
E-mail: hotel.de.l.elysee@wanadoo.fr

Madame Lafond

This solid-value, totally French hotel, comfortable and classical, will soon have a generous Napoleon III *salon* of great refinement. It already has hand-painted *faux marbre* staircase walls, a white marble fireplace, genuine antiques and many canopied beds. The basic intention is to make you feel at ease in a country-house environment with a few dramatically baroque details — a study of lamps and lights reveals some astounding gilded harvest sprays and spiky vegetables that look almost like prehistoric throwbacks. Otherwise, Jouy-pattern walls plus quilting, padding and plush are the thing. As usual, some 'standard' rooms are really quite small but there is always a moulded ceiling or hand-painted cupboard. There are fairly sombre rooms in shades of green, brown and beige, others are covered in bright flowers; the de luxe corner rooms are most attractive with three windows and space; top-floor junior suites have great character — sloping ceilings, timbers, nooks, pretty décor. A place of taste and comfort, it virtually faces the Ministry of the Interior's grand entrance so you always have a policeman at your door. Ask about long-stay terms for our readers.

Rooms: 32.
Price: Singles & doubles 780-1380 Frs
(€118.91-210.38); suites 1500 Frs.
Breakfast: Continental plus 65 Frs.
Meals: On request 80-170 Frs.
Metro: Champs Élysées, Madeleine,
Miromesnil.
RER: Opéra-Auber.
Bus routes: 28 32 49 52 80 83 93
Car park: Hôtel Bristol.

The 'tenant' of the Place Beauvau is Interior Minister and chief of police; *saussaie* comes from *saule* = birch. In the days of birching, did the police grow their own?

Entry No: 77   Map No: 1

Hôtel Élysées Matignon

3 rue de Ponthieu   **Tel:** (0)1 42 25 73 01
75008 Paris   **Fax:** (0)1 42 56 01 39
                                 E-mail: elyseesmatignon@wanadoo.fr

Alain Michaud & Jean-François Cornillot

Paris has more and more imitations of the 1920s Modern Style. The Matignon is superbly genuine 1924. Enter the rectangle-upon-rectangle porch, along the many-rectangled floor, stand under the perfect curves of the moulded ceiling light that grows out of those angles: you feel the message. You will be welcomed by people who are relaxed yet sensitive to your needs, a delightful contrast to the hustle of *Les Champs*. Every bedroom sports a large original fresco: landscapes or near-abstract still lifes, they are very proper given the original purpose of these rooms... Bathrooms have Art Deco mod cons and are being very fittingly renovated. Otherwise, there are discreet dark carpets, heavy curtains, co-ordinated quilted or textured bedcovers and head cushions (a bow to 90s fashion), black metal bedside lights (another), fine inner blinds and adequate storage. Rooms are not enormous but each has a little lobby for a sense of space. An evening venue for the Parisian 'in' crowd (11pm to dawn), the scarlet and black Mathis Bar puts on virginal white cloths for your breakfast — great fun, especially for night-lifers but bring earplugs if you plan to sleep early.

Rooms: 23.
Price: Single, double, suite 590-1200 Frs (€89.94-182.94).
Breakfast: 55 Frs.
Meals: On request 100-150 Frs.
Metro: Franklin Roosevelt.
RER: Charles de Gaulle-Étoile.
Bus routes: 28 32 42 49 73 93
Car park: Champs Elysées.

Mansions were built here in the 1700s (the Élysée Palace, for example, for Mme de Pompadour); in the 1800s, the 'Elysian Fields' were covered with modest houses; in the 1920s activity was less modest...

Map No: 1   **Entry No:** 78

Hôtel des Champs-Élysées

2 rue d'Artois
75008 Paris

Tel: (0)1 43 59 11 42
Fax: (0)1 45 61 00 61

Madame Monteil

Nothing is too much for Madame Monteil: the art of hospitality was inherited from her grandparents and parents, whose hotel this was; their delightful pre-war pictures hang here. An unpretentious façade speaks for the simple, gracious reception you will receive, in deep contrast with the nearby Champs Elysées vulgarity. And the new Art Deco mural in the *salon* is a triumph of taste and artistic talent. Each room has custom-made wooden furniture; covers and curtains are often English fabrics, subtly co-ordinated with pastel-pink, cream-sponged or turquoise walls for lighter or darker effect; wall-mounted bedside lights are clean-cut and well-placed and mirrored cupboards provide adequate storage. The small bathrooms have been recently renovated in smart grey, silver, black and white tiles or beige marble. Since this 'back' street may carry occasional posses of departing clubbers, all rooms (all but six give onto the street) are fully soundproofed and air-conditioned. With fresh baker's croissants and bread for breakfast, we thought we had found remarkable value in an expensive neighbourhood — and exceptional human contact.

Rooms: 36.
Price: Singles & doubles 500-600 Frs (€76.22-91.47); extra bed 80 Frs.
Breakfast: 45 Frs.
Meals: No.
Metro: St Philippe du Roule, Franklin Roosevelt.
RER: Charles de Gaulle-Étoile.
Bus routes: 22 28 32 73 80 83 93
Car park: Rue de Ponthieu.

Escape the frenzy: take one of the narrow alleys off Rue Washington and walk in the quiet, tree-shaded Cité Odiot — it has a slight feel of Georgian London.

Entry No: 79　　　　　　　　　　　　　　　　　　　　Map No: 1

Arc de Triomphe

•

Parc Monceau gardens

•

St Ferdinand

Étoile – Porte Maillot

 50 F

Hôtel Pergolèse

3 rue Pergolèse
75116 Paris

Tel: (0)1 53 64 04 04
Fax: (0)1 53 64 04 40
E-mail: hotel@pergolese.com
Web: www.hotelpergolese.com

Édith Vidalenc

The Arc de Triomphe is just here, yet once past the blue doors you enter a festival of contemporary design where light, materials (wood, leather, polished metal) and minute details all add up. Édith Vidalenc works with sought-after designer Rena Dumas to keep a sleek but warmly, curvaceously human hotel. Her sense of hospitality informs it all: the faithful team at reception are leagues away from the frostiness that can pass for 'four-star' treatment. Hilton McConnico did the pictures and the brilliant carpets in bar and *salons*. The leitmotiv is the entrance arch, repeated in leaf-like bedheads and sofas by curved patio windows. Pastel tones are mutedly smart so the multi-coloured breakfast room is a humorous wake-up nudge, the linen mats and fine silver a bow to tradition. Indeed, not taking oneself too seriously while doing a really professional job is the keynote here. Rooms, not vast but with good storage, are all similarly furnished in pale wood and leather with thick curtains and soft white bedcovers: no distracting patterns or prints. The star *Pergolèse* room (illustrated) is a small masterpiece in palest apricot with a few spots of colour and a superb open bathroom.

Rooms: 40.
Price: Single 1100-1500 Frs; double 1200-2000 Frs (€182.94-304.90).
Breakfast: Continental 75 Frs; buffet 100 Frs.
Meals: On request about 150 Frs
Metro: Argentine.
RER: & Air France bus: Porte Maillot.
Bus routes: 73 82
Car park: Place Saint Ferdinand.

Napoleon had the Arc de Triomphe built on this hill in honour of every single one of the 386 generals who fought in the Republican and Imperial wars: all their names are graven on't.

Entry No: 80   Map No: 1

Hôtel Résidence Impériale
155 avenue Malakoff
75116 Paris

Tel: (0)1 45 00 23 45
Fax: (0)1 45 01 88 82
E-mail: res.imperiale@wanadoo.fr
Web: www.paris-charming-hotels.com

Pierre Salles

A grand name but a most unsnooty hostelry: the young owner and his staff are enthusiastic, energetic, humorous and relaxed. Seeing how close it is to its huge neighbour, Paris's conference centre, it is inevitably prized by business and conference people but in no way do they impinge. Pierre Salles has renovated his hotel from top to bottom with double glazing, double windows and air conditioning — essential for rooms over the busy avenue — plus made-to-measure furniture in natural wood that make the best use of the space in each room. We particularly enjoyed the original lamps, like leather-covered urns, and their soft light. Beds are firm, upholstery richly quilted, curtains thickly generous, wallpaper unobtrusive. Top-floor rooms have timbers and sloping ceilings for a bit of character; those at the back look out over a row of small private gardens and a rather lovely old curved redbrick building. The *salon* has been most attractively done in brown, yellow and ivory, ideal for the paintings shown there, and the patio is perfect with its teak tables. If you are cooped up all day in the Palais des Congrès or arrive by airport bus at the Porte Maillot, this is a nearby haven.

Rooms: 37.
Price: Singles & doubles 740-920 Frs (€114.18-140.25); triples 890-1150 Frs.
Breakfast: Generous buffet 60 Frs.
Meals: On request 100-150 Frs.
Metro & RER & Air France bus: Porte Maillot.
Bus routes: 73 82 PC
Car park: Palais des Congrès.

Malakoff was a bastion at Sebastopol that fell to Marshal MacMahon in the Crimean War after he (not Julius Caesar) had declared famously *"J'y suis, j'y reste"*.

Map No: 1   **Entry No:** 81

Hôtel Centre Ville Étoile

6 rue des Acacias
75017 Paris

Tel: (0)1 58 05 10 00
Fax: (0)1 47 54 93 43
E-mail: hcv@centrevillehotels.com
Web: www.centrevillehotels.com

Alain Michaud & Idir Nasser

This tiny hotel has a definite style: for once, tiny has not meant cosy. I like it for its difference. The shiny black desk and the 20-foot ficus tree are in a three-storey galleried well of light — an ingenious and original space — that gives onto a plant-filled cul-de-sac where guests can sit out. The view from the top gallery, across metal frame and curtain wall, is an engineer's delight. The décor may be a little sombre for some; it is based on an Art Deco style that dictates the black and white theme, with a chromatic glance at American Surrealism in that original 1930s oil. There are prints from American cartoon strips and black/grey carpeting like running water. Rooms are small but spaces are well used, though storage remains limited. They can be masculine in brown and black with one red chair, or more pastelly, or elegant white, cream and grey. Bathrooms have white fittings, round basins, restful grey tiling, lots of mirrors, bathrobes. In contrast, bright red oriental-print cloths, black tables and airy Bauhaus wire chairs enliven the basement breakfast room. With so few rooms, staff have plenty of time to be friendly, helpful and really welcoming.

Rooms: 15.
Price: Singles & doubles 690-990 Frs (€105.19-150.92).
Breakfast: 60 Frs.
Meals: On request 100-150 Frs.
Metro: Argentine. **RER** & Air France bus: Charles de Gaulle-Étoile.
Bus routes: 43 73 92 93
Car park: 24 rue des Acacias.

In 1834, Louis Philippe's heir apparent took a fast bend nearby, fell out of his carriage and was killed. Banal? Perhaps, but few crash victims have Byzantine chapels built in their memory (St Ferdinand).

Entry No: 82   Map No: 1

Hôtel Régence Étoile

24 avenue Carnot   **Tel:** (0)1 58 05 42 42
75017 Paris   **Fax:** (0)1 47 66 78 86
                          E-mail: hotelregenceetoile-paris@gofornet.fr
                          Web: www.ou-dormir.fr/regence-etoile

Madame Montagnon

With its dressed stone façade onto one of the wide leafy avenues leading off the Arc de Triomphe, the Régence is an utterly Right Bank hoTel: smartly Empire, soberly businesslike, with a human touch. In the generous, marbled hallway, you will be greeted by a beautiful, naked and valuable statue; the big windows are hung with pale gold curtains, properly fringed and swagged, and that fascinating near-black marble fireplace demands closer inspection. Some nice furniture and atmospheric oils of 1890s Paris grace the panelled reception end where you may be greeted by a delightful bright young woman, or by the warm, knowledgeable and polyglot manageress. The corridors are elegantly blue and yellow and bedrooms are decorated with the same scheme: yellow walls, rich yellow damask curtains, blue carpets and quilted bedcovers. They are not huge but feel plush and reassuring with their solid, traditional-style, dark polished furniture and new ivory-tiled, marble-shelved bathrooms. Rooms on the front look through wrought-iron balconies and trees to the fine buildings opposite. You will be extremely comfortable here, and well received.

Rooms: 38.
Price: Singles & doubles 686-852 Frs (€104.58-129.89).
Breakfast: Buffet 50 Frs.
Meals: No.
Metro & RER: Charles de Gaulle-Etoile.
Bus routes: 22 30 31 43 52 73 92 93
Car park: Carnot.

The Arc de Triomphe, planned by Napoleon but finished long after his fall from glory into miserable death, is 50 metres high. The view of the avenues radiating off this *étoile* is superb.

Map No: 1   **Entry No:** 83

Étoile Park Hôtel

10 avenue MacMahon
75017 Paris

Tel: (0)1 42 67 69 63
Fax: (0)1 43 80 18 99
E-mail: ephot@easynet.fr
Web: www.hotel-etoilepark.com

Sylviane Leridon

This Haussmann-style building and the wide leafy avenue under its windows were built in the 1860s and No 10 has been an hotel, belonging to the same family, ever since. From some of the rooms they say you can see the sun rise over the Arc de Triomphe... and it's a splendid sight up there, proud and solid with its magnificent sculptures. In the short time she has been here, Madame Leridon has, with enthusiasm and taste, transformed the sitting area into a warm, unfussy 1930s space, in complete contrast with the grand exterior: natural materials — wood and stone, leather and linen — in plain colours, well-made artificial bouquets and very real cacti, and super pictures by Hilton McConnico (not 1930s). Round the corner is the bar with a discreet television set and the Internet Machine (cards for sale) then, further still, the delightful breakfast room with lively deck-chair-stripe seating and a smooth modern buffet bar. For the moment, the bedrooms are less exciting, even somewhat spartan in their sobriety as they wait for renewal. Colour schemes are pale yellow, brown, ivory and dark blue, bathrooms are fine and good engravings hang on the walls. Well-placed and very welcoming.

Rooms: 28.
Price: Singles & doubles 520-850 Frs (€79.27-129.58).
Breakfast: In room 45 Frs; buffet 65 Frs.
Meals: On request 100-200 Frs.
Metro & RER: Charles de Gaulle-Etoile.
Bus routes: 30 31 73 92 93
Car park: MacMahon.

Of great Irish descendence, MacMahon was utterly French in his accumulation of military and political glories and their titles, finishing as President of the Republic in 1873.

Entry No: 84

Map No: 1

Hôtel Princesse Caroline

1bis rue Troyon
75017 Paris

Tel: (0)1 58 05 30 00/
         (0)1 43 80 62 20
Fax: (0)1 42 27 49 53
E-mail: contact@princessecaroline.fr
Web: www.hotelprincessecaroline.fr

Monsieur Lascaux

This princess has had a radical facelift, inside and out: her fine 1920s façade has been cleaned and repaired, her rooms completely rethought, her ground floor transformed into a series of small sitting corners in warm, contemporary comfort. A stone's throw from the Arc de Triomphe, here is up-to-date traditional French style. Nothing swirly here, no frills: lines are clean, fabrics are luxuriously soft damask, bathrooms are done in rather lovely Italian marbles and all the richly polished furniture — bedheads and side tables, upholstered chairs — was made to measure in Italy. Three or four pleasing colour schemes (blue/yellow, ginger/yellow, orange/grey) are followed throughout and copies of Old Masters hang on the walls. The big junior suites have cushions to soften the expanse of bed and fitted carpets with 'woven-in' rugs; a few of the splendid original carved fireplaces with great mirrors are still here, a little statue gracing each one. It is all very new, bedding is superb, the bronze lamps really heavy. In the basement, breakfast in a warmly classical Mediterranean-hued room with the Grand Canal on the wall. A place of unostentatious style and real comfort.

Rooms: 53.
Price: Singles & doubles 975-1385 Frs
(€148.64-211.14).
Breakfast: Buffet 75 Frs.
Meals: No.
Metro & RER: Charles de Gaulle-Etoile.
Bus routes: 30 31 92 93
Car park: MacMahon.

Caroline Bonaparte married a publican's son turned soldier; her Emperor brother Napoleon made him King of Naples; then she persuaded him to discard imperial domination — and he ended before a firing squad.

Map No: 1

Entry No: 85

Hôtel Tilsitt Étoile
23 rue Brey
75017 Paris

Tel: (0)1 43 80 39 71
Fax: (0)1 47 66 37 63
E-mail: info@tilsitt.com
Web: www.tilsitt.com

Christine Lafosse &
Stéphanie Batten

The atmosphere at the Tilsitt is convivial and friendly, the rooms are discreet and sober, owners and staff are direct, natural and charming — nothing to scare or surprise you here. It is a fine old Parisian building: the very beautiful original front doors have had to come off for the sake of hotel access but have been placed lovingly on show behind the reception desk and the old panelling still gives the lobby and sitting space much muted elegance. This pink-cushioned, green-dhurried *salon* looks onto a dear little mossy patio and when you descend to the broad, vaulted breakfast basement you find more ivy peeking in as well as light from a well to the street. Some bedrooms, including the big family rooms, also wear green and pink with a dash of yellow here and there: all very fresh and light. Other rooms are simpler, all have ivory-coloured walls that set off the intriguing framed copies of pages from century-old make-up catalogues. Bathrooms are serenely grey and white with good fittings and mirrors. This is a thoroughly restful place to stay just down from the Arc de Triomphe and people want you to feel at home here.

Rooms: 38, including 2 family rooms.
Price: Singles & doubles 650-1000 Frs (€99.09-152.45).
Breakfast: Buffet 65 Frs.
Meals: No.
Metro & RER: Charles de Gaulle-Etoile.
Bus routes: 30 31 43 92 93
Car park: Avenue de Wagram.

The whole of the *Étoile* is ringed with memories of Napoleon's great deeds: Tilsitt is the Prussian town where he signed a peace treaty in 1807 with Russian and Prussia.

Entry No: 86   Map No: 1

Hôtel Flaubert
19 rue Rennequin
75017 Paris

Tel: (0)1 46 22 44 35
Fax: (0)1 43 80 32 34
Web: www.hotelflaubert.com

Monsieur & Madame
Schneider

The eager and active new owners have undertaken a brightening campaign here, so vibrant blue and yellow or crimson and paisley march alongside each other — a real improvement. Bedroom furniture is still Italian wicker — light and not at all overbearing; there is always a table and one or two chairs or a stool. Much attention has been paid to details like lighting and new tap fittings. Bathrooms are good and the larger rooms have plenty of storage. The Schneiders are also tending the Flaubert's surpassing asset: its miniature jungle, a long courtyard between two parts of the building connected by wooden stairs and bridges festooned with flowers and greenery. This could be the depths of Normandy, the great Gustave Flaubert's home county, and it is most un-Parisian to walk through the bushes and up the outside stairs to a room under the eaves (or you can take the lift, of course). The breakfast room, with its big windows onto the street and yet more green life, has bent-wood chairs, floral cushions and Provençal floor tiles to prolong the country feel, and there's a pretty new sitting space by the other window. Altogether excellent value.

Rooms: 40.
Price: Singles & doubles 510-600 Frs (€77.75-91.47).
Breakfast: Buffet: 48 Frs.
Meals: No.
Metro: Ternes, Pereire.
RER: Pereire, Charles de Gaulle-Étoile.
Bus routes: 30 31 43 84 92 93
Car park: Fiat opposite hotel.

In 1682, Rennequin built the magnificent *Machine de Marly* which, for 120 years, propelled water up to the great fountains at Versailles using 14 wheels and 221 pumps.

Map No: 1   **Entry No: 87**

Hôtel Eber Monceau

18 rue Léon Jost
75017 Paris

Tel: (0)1 46 22 60 70
Fax: (0)1 47 63 01 01

Jean-Marc Eber

Jean-Marc Eber instantly communicates his enthusiasm and his pleasure in welcoming guests: a lighthearted approach married to very professional management. And the wonderfully quiet Eber is a *Relais Silence*. You may meet top models, fashion designers or other film folk appropriate to this smart neighbourhood. The fascinating process of building the Statue of Liberty, made in a nearby yard, is illustrated on the walls. And you can borrow a house umbrella in your hour of need — a superior touch, perhaps inspired by the two umbrella-toting braves on the mantelpiece? The intimate bar area is a good place for breakfast, served any time with 15 sorts of jam and three teas. Rooms vary in size, some are quite small, some have grandly high ceilings; the duplexes are large enough for families and the one with private terrace is particularly seductive. Fairly neutral colour schemes with pastel print curtains and covers, strengthened by the occasional dark splash, make them all very restful. Nice old mirrors, the odd carved armoire, bring a touch of the antique; storage space is generally adequate; bathrooms are pleasingly tiled. A delightful yet professional host, too.

Rooms: 18.
Price: Singles & doubles 710-880 Frs (€108.24-134.16); family 1300 Frs; duplex 1400-1500 Frs.
Breakfast: 70 Frs.
Meals: On request about 170 Frs.
Metro: Courcelles.
RER: Charles de Gaulle-Étoile, Pereire.
Bus routes: 30 84
Car park: 200m Elf garage.

Nearby, do visit the two little-known, superbly-furnished mansion museums, treasure houses of French design and taste: Nissim de Camondo and Jacquemart André.

Entry No: 88   Map No: 1

Hôtel Médéric

4 rue Médéric
75017 Paris

Tel: (0)1 47 63 69 13
Fax: (0)1 44 40 05 33

Bernard Rolin

In a residential area near smart Parc Monceau and the Champs Élysées, the Médéric is run by a really hospitable brother and sister team. Madame, the most elegant, friendly, Parisienne grandmother imaginable, says you should use hotels as you use the theatre: for something you wouldn't find at home. So, making the most of the small rooms and banal built-in units that were there, the Rolins have put gilt-bronze lights over the beds (spiky flower sprays or swirly-stemmed wheels that make you laugh outright with delight), a fine old mirror in each room, a very French armchair wherever possible. Rooms are mostly small, bathrooms adequate, shower rooms tiny, but the two top-floor rooms, with sloping ceilings, roof windows and skirted tables, can take three or four. Lit by a baroque torch-bearing servant boy, the sitting corner is most attractive, with its deep grey plush sofa, a couple of moss-green armchairs, a red-skirted table: like a French family *salon*; the grey and yellow dining room is charming and a mirror reflects it all back, doubling the depth. A friendly, intimate, good-value two-star with "the best beds in Paris" (said a regular guest I met there).

Rooms: 27, including 2 suites.
Price: Singles & doubles 450-625 Frs (€68.6-95.28); suites 900 Frs.
Breakfast: 45 Frs.
Meals: No.
Metro: Courcelles.
RER: Charles de Gaulle-Etoile.
Bus routes: 30 84
Car park: Rue de Courcelles.

Nearby Avenue de Wagram is named after an Austrian village where Napoleon won a 'resounding victory' over the Archduke — 20 000 dead versus 22 000. Howzat!

Map No: 1

Entry No: 89

 30 F

 som

Hôtel de Banville

166 boulevard Berthier
75017 Paris

Tel: (0)1 42 67 70 16
Fax: (0)1 44 40 42 77
E-mail: hotelbanville@wanadoo.fr
Web: www.hotelbanville.fr

Marianne Moreau

A deliciously Parisian hotel, with the elegance of inherited style, soft and welcoming like a private home. The family (third generation now) love their *métier* and make their own pâté for light suppers. In the gracious *salon*, the bar, deep sofas and piano are supervised by elaborately-framed Old Masters. The Moreaus' latest bedroom designs are wondrous. 'Marie', in stone and earth tones — palest eggshell to rich red loam — has a gauzily-canopied bed, a sweet little terrace (Eiffel Tower view) and a brilliant bathroom with thick curtains for soft partitioning; 'Amélie', sunnily feminine in pale yellow and soft ginger, rejoices in her own balcony; the three 'Pastourelles' are prettily countrified with fresh gingham and old wood; 'Banville' is another exceptional mix of modern comforts, warm fabrics and history-laden wood. Behind beautifully curtained screens, their bathrooms are a delight. The other rooms, beautifully filled with light, pale colours and intimacy, have a gentle, airy touch, period and modern furniture, good bathrooms. Staff are charming — the house motto might be "Know your guests' wishes before they do". *Good public transport to all parts of Paris.*

Rooms: 38.
Price: Singles & doubles 810-1550 Frs
(€123.48-236.3).
Breakfast: Continental plus 70 Frs.
Meals: Light meals 50-150 Frs.
Metro: Porte de Champerret, Pereire.
RER: Pereire.
Bus routes: 92 84 93 PC
Car Park: Rue de Courcelles.

Théodore de Banville, a 19th-century poet who was neither a materialist nor a romantic, had a noble passion: "to clothe my ideas in a perfect form of beauty and technical mastery".

Entry No: 90

Map No: 1

Hôtel de Neuville

3 rue Verniquet
75017 Paris

Tel: (0)1 43 80 26 30
Fax: (0)1 43 80 38 55
E-mail: neuville@hotellerie.net

Michel Caron

 60 Frs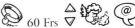

Its 19th-century geranium-decked façade overlooks a quiet square. You will be welcomed by young and enthusiastic staff in the large, airy, split-level lobby where light floods in through the arched windows. It feels like a club with oak-tinted armchairs, low tables, bar stools and interesting contemporary paintings. Beyond the two pairs of Ionic columns a little green, flowering patio gives a sense of space and peace to the deep-seated *salon*. And the basement breakfast room has a wonderful surprise: the patio is down here too, the green light and air skillfully augmented with mirrors. The bedrooms over the boulevard are a good size and from the top floors you can see bits of the Sacré Coeur. Other rooms are smaller and darker but the two with frothily canopied beds are so delightful one forgets their size; others like this are planned. Colours are soft orange with salmon pink in bold chintzes, paisleys or gentle florals; the furniture is comfortable with some brass bedsteads, some plain pine; there is decent storage space, the occasional antique mirror, old lamps and prints from Old Masters to balance the modern art downstairs. A quiet, friendly place to stay. I find the atmosphere most relaxing.

Rooms: 28.
Price: Singles & doubles 750-850 Frs (€114.34-129.58); extra bed 150 Frs.
Breakfast: Buffet 55 Frs.
Meals: On request 100-200 Frs.
Metro & RER: Pereire.
Bus routes: 84 92 93
Car park: Hotel or Boulevard Berthier.

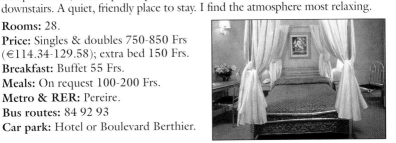

Edme Verniquet was an architect but he is essentially remembered for the superb map of Paris in 72 huge sheets that he finished in 1799, after working at it for 28 years.

Hôtel Jardin de Villiers

18 rue Claude Pouillet
75017 Paris

Tel: (0)1 42 67 15 60
Fax: (0)1 42 67 32 11
E-mail: hoteljdv@minitel.net
Web: www.123france.com/jdv

Daniela Riederich & Pierre Bachy

The little street is wonderfully quiet but just round the corner is lively Rue de Lévis where one of Paris's typical street markets is held every day: pedestrians only and shops all spreading their wares onto the pavement. Your charming, multi-lingual hosts are recent converts to the hotel business, and seem pretty good at it — their attitude to guests is quietly open and easy. So is the generous ground-floor space, where you see straight through the attractively unpompous red and yellow sitting area to the *jardin*. You can sit out in this sheltered courtyard under the tall tree and have a leisurely breakfast, or in the stone-vaulted basement room where the owner's excellent travel photographs hang. They have decorated their hotel in a different basic colour per floor: green, blue, yellow, dark blue (there are only four storeys), the furniture is all French rosewood veneer — light and decorative -, the fabrics are fresh florals and stripes, bathrooms are modern and good. It is a comfortable, honest place where service is a priority and peace is assured. *Very attractive price for our readers.*

Rooms: 26.
Price: For ASP readers: 600-750 Frs (€91.47-114.34).
Breakfast: Continental plus 40 Frs.
Meals: On request 100-150 Frs.
Metro: Villiers.
RER: Opéra-Auber.
Bus routes: 30 53 94
Car park: Consult hotel.

Poullet, good at physics, was made Head of the *Arts et Métiers* in 1840 but, poor at politics, he was fired for 'lack of enthusiasm' regarding the 1848 uprising.

Entry No: 92   Map No: 1

Opéra – Grands Boulevards

New Orient Hôtel
16 rue de Constantinople
75008 Paris

Tel: (0)1 45 22 21 64
Fax: (0)1 42 93 83 23
E-mail: new.orient.hotel@wanadoo.fr
Web: www.adx.fr/new-orient-hotel

Catherine & Sepp Wehrlé

A real find near the Gare St Lazare, the New Orient (Constantinople may have something to do with the name) is pretty, original and fun. Behind a bottle-green frontage flanked by carriage lamps and ivy geraniums pouring off the windowsills, the warm, attractive owners display their love of trawling through country-house sales for furniture, pictures and mirrors and the mix of styles is sheer delight — Louis XVI, 1900s, Art Deco,... they want it to feel like home. The ground floor houses a painted telephone box and a carved dresser, a piano and a set of light country watercolours. In the breakfast area, a fine grandfather clock stands beside pink/green-clothed rattan tables and a real bar where people sit on stools and chat over coffee. You get the feel of the rooms from the landings where a bottle-green carpet underscores green doors with red mouldings: full of character. There are brass beds and carved beds, one with little columns, one with superb inlay and matching dressing table; there are pretty little tables everywhere and bright oriental or Mediterranean fabrics. Bathrooms are in pristine white square tiles. Huge charm, excellent value, remarkably likeable people.

Rooms: 30.
Price: Singles & doubles 415-630 Frs
(€63.27-96.04).
Breakfast: 40 Frs.
Meals: No.
Metro: Villiers, Europe.
RER: Opéra-Auber.
Bus routes: 30 53
Car park: Europe.

In the Musée d'Orsay is Monet's unforgettable painting of the Gare St Lazare, flooded with steam and smoke and blurred blue light. It caused a scandal at the time as 'an inappropriate subject'.

Entry No: 93

Map No: 1

Le Lavoisier
21 rue Lavoisier
75008 Paris

Tel: (0)1 53 30 06 06
Fax: (0)1 53 30 23 00
E-mail: hotel@lavoisier.com
Web: www.hotellavoisier.com

Ludovic Peressini

The plainly engraved name on the white stone of the façade sets the tone: the newly-renovated Lavoisier is beautiful and entirely frill-less and as you step through the door the bustle of the streets dims into the distance. Here is the casual elegance of muted warm colours, fine natural materials and original portraits. Antiques and modern pieces sit well together, squidgy sofas lie alongside wrought-iron banisters, a dark and intimate bar hides at the back — you will find it tempting for a pre-dinner drink. Traditional, with the designer touch of custom-made black wooden furniture plus the odd clever *brocante* find, the good-sized bedrooms are immaculate, their tall windows clothed in thick, rich curtains, their bathrooms perfect in grey marble and white china with deep moulded friezes. Staff are young, eager and helpful, fresh flowers on the reception desk and plenty of towels in the bathroom are welcome sights after a day in the city and although daytime traffic noise cannot be entirely kept out, the double glazing is good and the little street is quiet at night — no raucous bars or late-night cafés. A thoroughly civilised place, twinned with the St Grégoire and the Tourville.

Rooms: 30, including 2 junior suites.
Price: Singles, doubles, suites 1290-2500 Frs (€196.66-381.12).
Breakfast: Continental plus 70 Frs.
Meals: On request 100-200 Frs.
Metro: St Augustin.
RER: Opéra-Auber
Bus routes: 32 84
Car park: Nearby consult hotel.

Do walk to Place de la Madeleine and visit the most amazing public lavatories in Paris: Art Nouveau moulded doors and stained-glass windows, all hidden beneath the pavement there.

Map No: 1   **Entry No:** 94

Hôtel Newton Opéra

11 bis rue de l'Arcade
75008 Paris

Tel: (0)1 42 65 32 13
Fax: (0)1 42 65 30 90
E-mail: newtonopera@easynet.fr
Web: www.hotel-newton-opera.com

Monsieur Simian & Madame Tobrouki

Those little attentions that count: a pretty flask of mandarine liqueur and two tiny goblets in your room, a superbly finished bathroom in grey pinstripe tiling, makeup remover pads, a magnifying mirror. On a quiet street, not far from Paris's renowned department stores, the Newton Opéra will enfold you in soft, peaceful elegance. The big *salon* is peach plush with period pieces on oriental rugs: a good place to read the papers; the breakfast room is a classic stone vault with high-backed chairs, a generous buffet, and prints that remind us of the artistic heyday of the 1900s. Bedrooms are not big but very attractive in their colourful dress of sunshine yellow, peach pink or cool blue, the furniture Louis XVI or polished rustic with a lyre-back chair or two, a long gilt-framed mirror... and a modem socket. Two rooms have private, shrubbed balconies with tables and loungers; book early, they are much coveted. Or try the bargain weekend offer with room, champagne and a night out in the price. As a loyal Egyptian client told me: "The room is deliciously cosy, the bathroom has everything you need and they are so friendly — I come for several weeks every year". *Internet access on ground floor.*

Rooms: 31.
Price: Single, double, triple 860-980-1060 Frs (€131.11-161.60).
Breakfast: Buffet 60 Frs.
Meals: On request 100-300 Frs.
Metro: Madeleine, Havre-Caumartin.
RER: Auber.
Bus routes: 22 27 42 52 53 66
Roissybus
Car park: Rue Chauveau Lagarde.

La Madeleine took time to find its religious feet: started in 1764, stopped during the Revolution, named Temple of Fame by Napoleon, it was finally consecrated in 1842.

Entry No: 95   Map No: 1

Hôtel des Croisés

63 rue St Lazare
75009 Paris

Tel: (0)1 48 74 78 24
Fax: (0)1 49 95 04 43

Madame Bojena

Not a single crusader (*croisé*) in sight, but one can well believe that the thick-carpeted, finely-carved stone and timber hallway was built as a bank in 1870. It soon became an hotel, and has never looked back. The best rooms carry wonderful legacies of those days of rich dark furniture and log fires: ceramic and marble fireplaces, superbly-crafted cupboards, inlaid beds, carved alcoves — one room even has a 'gazebo'. Not all rooms are as spectacular but choice ornaments are placed here and there and bathrooms are fine, some enormous. Curtains and bedding fit too: heavy velvets, lots of red, some pretty pastel piqués. In the attractive yellow and green breakfast room there's yet another fireplace, two interesting 19th-century busts on the well-garnished buffet table, wicker furniture and a lovely antique bird cage housing two plaster birds — a nice gesture. The owner wants deeply to keep the building's historical character (others would have ripped out all that old stuff ages ago), only looking for furniture with 1900-1930 lines. Madame Bojena, a gentle and efficient presence, has known and loved the hotel for years. There's double glazing, and the traffic dies down after 8pm.

Rooms: 27, including 3 suites.
Price: Singles & doubles 435-650 Frs (€66.32-99.09); extra bed 95 Frs.
Breakfast: Buffet 40 Frs.
Meals: No.
Metro: Trinité d'Estienne d'Orves.
RER: Opéra-Auber.
Bus routes: 26 32 42 43 68 81
Car park: 300m: consult hotel.

The Trinité church, built in 1867 by Ballu, is pure 19th-century Paris in its imitative 16th-century Florentine style and its 65-metre tower that lines up with the Sacré Cœur — a real landmark.

Map No: 2

Entry No: 96

Hôtel Favart

5 rue de Marivaux   **Tel:** (0)1 42 97 59 83
75002 Paris   **Fax:** (0)1 40 15 95 58

Éric Champetier

The Favart's big public rooms are splendidly pure Paris with their columns, velvet and curly wrought-iron stair rail — right and proper, given its highly-decorated neo-classical neighbour, the Opéra Comique (Salle Favart). The breakfast room beyond the lobby is also greenly grand and mirrored and rich-feeling. But the people who greet you are utterly unpretentious and friendly: one understands why a cosmopolitan collection of clients returns generation after generation. Good-sized bedrooms, some still being renovated, are basically classic in style with reproduction furniture, plush upholstery, draped curtains, moiré wallpaper. On the first floor over the street you have the privilege of living under original beams and behind those gently arched windows (admire the glazier's art here) that face the rising sun and the Salle Favart; and all is quiet once the theatre-goers have left. Even the bathrooms have character, some almost completely lined with mirrors, another done with amazing blue water-blotch and tiny-flower tiles. Comfort, character and a sense of service are the keynotes here, in among the great theatres and the much-sung boulevards.

Rooms: 37.
Price: Singles & doubles 540-800 Frs
(€82.32-121.96), including breakfast.
Breakfast: Included.
Meals: No.
Metro: Richelieu-Drouot.
RER: Opéra-Auber.
Bus routes: 20 39 48
Car park: Boulevard des Italiens.

Having started life as a pastry-cook, 18th-century dramatic author Charles Simon Favart created the musical comedy (yes, Gilbert and Sullivan) and was hugely popular for half a century.

Entry No: 97   Map No: 2

Hôtel Chopin

10 boulevard Montmartre
(46 passage Jouffroy)
75009 Paris

Tel: (0)1 47 70 58 10
Fax: (0)1 42 47 00 70

Philippe Bidal

 quiet

History is here. Built in 1846 in a typical Parisian shopping arcade, the Chopin has always been an hotel, the great green pot planted in the airy lobby since Chinoiserie was 'in'. Smiles are freely given, people are pleased to see you, but pianists beware — the piano hasn't been tuned for years. Unusually quiet, all rooms give onto courtyards and low rooftops, the most stunning being the zinc expanses over the waxworks museum (sleep deeply above bloody scenes of French Revolution): the *Salle des Papillons* looks like a medieval apsed chapel, the glass roof of the arcade like a vast upturned hull. Most rooms are a good size for the price; bathrooms are modern, simple and functional — one has a tiny attic *boudoir* with chair. Stairs and corridors are elegant with rich green carpet, salmon grasspaper walls, nicely-framed prints and some fine table lamps. Bedrooms have vibrant colour schemes (deep salmon, bright yellow or raspberry walls, rich green carpets and matching upholstery), simple, pretty furniture and firm foam mattresses. Monsieur Bidal's grandmother's water colours add class to the welcoming breakfast room of this supremely friendly, good-value hotel.

Rooms: 36, including 2 singles with separate wc.
Price: Single, double, triple 405-595 Frs (€61.74-90.71).
Breakfast: Continental buffet 40 Frs.
Meals: No.
Metro: Richelieu-Drouot, Grands Boulevards. **RER:** Opéra-Auber.
Bus routes: 49 67 74 85
Car park: Rue Chauchat.

There are some fascinating trades in the *passage* — an antique walking stick specialist, for example — and people offer walking tours of the arcades, ancestors of the shopping mall.

Map No: 2   **Entry No: 98**

 60 F

Hôtel Pulitzer Opéra

23 rue du Faubourg Montmartre
75009 Paris

Tel: (0)1 53 34 98 10
Fax: (0)1 53 34 00 07
E-mail: pulitzer@free.fr

Yolande Herrero

You may get a hint of the inside from the well-planted black marble window boxes that line the pavement outside, but the contrast between the noisy, colourful, car-hooting, populous shopping and cabaret scene on the street and the interior of the Pulitzer, full of space and light and peace, is almost miraculous. It is modern, beautiful and streamlined. The impeccably parqueted and columned hallway leads through to an inner courtyard garden between the two buildings and announces the style immediately: the feel of a yacht, wood all over, interesting lighting. It is clean-cut, sober and warm. The sitting spaces offer simple, square armchairs and interesting collages in pine picture frames. Upstairs, where half the rooms give onto the street and half onto the courtyard, the approaches are quietly smart blue and grey. Bedrooms have pale yellow sponged walls and striking redwood panels behind beds, some of them extending into alcove storage spaces. Bedcovers and curtains are dark green with gold fleck, again, warm and unfussily comforting. Bathrooms, perfect in eau-de-nil and pale sage, have proper mirrors and shelf space. And of course, soundproofing is excellent.

Rooms: 44.
Price: Singles & doubles 950-1600 Frs
(€144.83-243.92).
Breakfast: Buffet 70 Frs.
Meals: On request.
Metro: Grands Boulevards.
RER: Opéra-Auber.
Bus routes: 74
Car park: Drouot.

Contrary to general belief, the Grands Boulevards were not Haussmann's doing: it was Louis XIV who tore down part of Paris to open these avenues for his chattering, strolling courtiers.

Entry No: 99

Map No: 2

Villa Fénelon
23 rue Buffault
75009 Paris

Tel: (0)1 48 78 32 18
Fax: (0)1 48 78 38 15

Éric Champetier

Villa is the right word here, a big one: country has come to town in the form of a wonderful shrubbery between the two 19th-century townhouses that make up the hotel. From the street you enter what was the great carriage porch, framed by its pilastered arches, now walled with mirrors and leading to the old stable yard, now the garden. Soft lighting, comfortable armchairs and oriental rugs soften the space; there's another more intimate *salon* onto the street, one dark blue and gold breakfast space beyond it and another with wooden garden furniture, a big rich tapestry and a big window over the garden. The pleasing rooms are furnished in repro Louis XVI and a motley choice of colour schemes in florals and stripes: quite a lot of pale tangerine and ginger, giving lift and personality, mirrors on cupboard doors, bathrooms, some with more mirror panels, that could do with refreshing. The little street is quiet — there's a synagogue opposite — though two main thoroughfares pass nearby so there could be distant traffic noise. It feels very peaceful and welcoming inside. Delightful staff, pretty remarkable value, and convenient for the Gare du Nord too.

Rooms: 38.
Price: Singles & doubles 410-570 Frs (€62.50-86.90), including breakfast.
Breakfast: Included.
Meals: No.
Metro: Cadet, Le Peletier, Notre Dame de Lorette.
RER: Opéra-Auber, Gare du Nord.
Bus routes: 26 32 42 43 67 74 85
Car park: Rue Mayran.

Archbishop Fénelon, a brilliant teacher and preacher, was described by Sainte Beuve as "That tall, thin, big-nosed man with eyes whence fire and spirit flow in torrents".

Map No: 2

Entry No: 100

Ils ne savent où donner de la tête
They don't know which way to turn

Elle a fondu dans ses bras
She melted in his arms

Sacré Coeur
•
Place du Tertre & artists
•
Montmartre cemetery
•
Moulin Rouge
•
Funicular railway

Montmartre

Hôtel Le Bouquet de Montmartre

1 rue Durantin   **Tel:** (0)1 46 06 87 54
75018 Paris   **Fax:** (0)1 46 06 09 09
                                Web: www.bouquet-de-montmartre.com

Jennifer Gibergues

The Bouquet de Montmartre certainly lives up to its name (origin unknown) — sweet, flowery and boudoir-like. A good two-star hotel, it may not be to everyone's taste but it is all-of-a-piece, a lesson in a particular type of French interior. The life-size uniformed butler and the black and white mosaic floor amaze the eye; the décor is flock 'brocade' wallpaper, glue-on mouldings and curlicues, curvy sideboards and Louis XVI chairs. This careful decoration covers the stairs and landings where the original 1920s banisters are painted white and gold to match and all doors are padded. The rooms vary in size and shape but the design principle is beds in alcoves with myriad little cupboards around and candle-shaped lights. There's the odd plastic cherub bas-relief too. The newer bath/shower rooms are smartly done in two-coloured mosaic tiling and the recent mattresses are firm foam. The delightful Gibergues family work hard at keeping up with their large household and still have time to sit and chat with their guests. Friendly, simple, in one of the prettiest squares in Paris (a meeting place for all sorts and conditions of local *braves*) and excellent value.

Rooms: 36.
Price: Singles & doubles 410-520 Frs (€62.50-79.27).
Breakfast: 30 Frs.
Meals: No.
Metro: Abbesses (take lift up to street, not stairs).
RER: Gare du Nord.
Bus routes: 30 54 67 68 74 80 95
Car park: Place de Clichy.

You emerge from the metro at Abbesses under one of the finest remaining Art Nouveau canopies by Hector Guimard, deliciously blending into its leafy surroundings.

Entry No: 101   Map No: 2

 small

Hôtel Prima Lepic

29 rue Lepic
75018 Paris

Tel: (0)1 46 06 44 64
Fax: (0)1 46 06 66 11
E-mail: reservation@hotel-prima-lepic.com

Martine Bourgeon

All the rooms in this warren of a place, built round three little courtyards, are differently, deliciously countrified — it's like staying at grandmama's cottage: light flowery wallpapers, lace and bows, draped canopies and little old tables. But the brilliant murals downstairs are pure Montmartre: basilica, cabarets, local characters keep you company as you have breakfast or afternoon tea on cast-iron conservatory furniture among the plant life. The hotel is local too: balustrades, floors and doors following the hillside at all angles, village life bustling among the little shops outside. The new owners, passionate about the Lepic, are redecorating in all faithfulness to the country inn theme — brass lamps and big gilt-framed mirrors for ever — while the new bathrooms, still smallish and functional but much more up to date, are definitely an improvement. The largest rooms (ending in 5) have grand double doors, two windows, perhaps a balcony with long long view to the Right Bank or a marble fireplace... But other rooms are good value too. And afternoon teas are planned for winter-time, with the occasional home-made cake for weary travellers. An excellent place with delightful staff.

Rooms: 38, including 3 apartments.
Price: Singles & doubles 400-450 Frs
(€60.98-68.6); apartments 620-850 Frs.
Breakfast: 40 Frs.
Meals: On request 150-200 Frs;
afternoon tea served.
Metro: Blanche, Abbesses.
RER: Gare du Nord.
Bus routes: 30 54 68 74
Car park: 100m: consult hotel.

General Lepic knew how to follow the wind of fortune: he fought brilliantly for Napoleon and was made a Baron, then turned royalist and was made a Count by King Louis XVIII.

Map No: 2

Entry No: 102

Le Caulaincourt Square Hôtel

2 square Caulaincourt
63/65 rue Caulaincourt
75018 Paris

Tel: (0)1 46 06 46 06
Fax: (0)1 46 06 46 16
E-mail: bonjour@caulaincourt.com
Web: www.caulaincourt.com

Monsieur Hacène

Paris-by-the-Seine can be sweltering and unbreathable; come perch on this airy hillside. The hotel gives onto two slopes — one of those vertiginous staircases on one side and a scruffy, woody slope of communal space at the back. It is a basic place to stay in an exquisitely privileged position. The 'mountain air' sweeps through the warren-like corridors from the garden, also a blessed source of quiet (except when the teenagers next door blast a momentary techno-rave over their mammoth decibel machines, but this is short-lived). This is the peaceful, bourgeois part of Montmartre yet you can walk up to the Sacré Cœur in five minutes. The lobby and breakfast room, directly off the leafy impasse (where there's an excellent café-restaurant) are as straightforward as the rest. Most rooms are plainly furnished with decent firm bedding, candlewick bedcovers, very adequate bedside lights and showers and neutral wallpapers but the new owners are giving it a more contemporary look with blue and ivory striped wallpaper and colourful tiled shower rooms. Few frills, but really excellent value and good, friendly service (radical plans suggest a lift). *Internet access on ground floor.*

Rooms: 50.
Price: Singles & doubles 280-350 Frs (€42.69-53.36); triples 330-370 Frs.
Breakfast: Buffet 28 Frs.
Meals: No.
Metro: Lamarck-Caulaincourt.
RER: Gare du Nord.
Bus routes: 80
Car park: Place de Clichy.

An aristocrat who renounced his peerage, Caulaincourt was a foot soldier during the Revolution, an ardent follower of Napoleon, a friend of Tsar Alexander, and still managed to die in his bed.

Entry No: 103

Map No: 2

Useful vocabulary

Some useful words and expressions to help you avoid ending up like this:

Bolster/Pillow	*Un Traversin/Un Oreiller*
Blanket	*Une Couverture*
Towel	*Une Serviette*
Tea; herb tea	*Un Thé; Une Infusion*
Ice	*De la glace*
Ice-cream; Mirror	*Une Glace*
Glass	*Un Verre*
Coat hangers	*Des Cintres*
Light bulb; Blister	*Une Ampoule*
Sticking plaster	*Du Sparadrap*
Soap; Shampoo	*Du Savon; Du Shampooing*
Lavatory paper	*Du Papier toilette*
Fan	*Un Ventilateur*
Out of order/broken	*En panne/cassé*
Stuck	*Coincé*

Paumé
Dropout; lost case

The room is too small/big/ *La chambre est trop petite/grande*
noisy/quiet/expensive/cheap. *bruyante/tranquille/chère/bon marché.*
May I please have a pillow? *Je voudrais un oreiller, s'il vous plaît.*
May I leave my children/wife/ *Pourrais-je laisser mes enfants/ma femme/*
husband with the concierge? *mon mari avec le concierge?*
I can't open the window. *Je n'arrive pas à ouvrir la fenêtre.*
Where can I get some fresh air? *Où peut-on trouver un peu d'air?*
May I have a room over the *Je voudrais une chambre sur*
garden/courtyard? *le jardin/la cour.*
Get out of my room! *Sortez de ma chambre!*
Leave me alone! *Laissez-moi tranquille!*
Is this really tea? *C'est vraiment du thé ça?*
The shower/bath/loo is blocked. *La douche/la baignoire/le wc est bouché.*
My wallet/key/baby is locked *J'ai enfermé mon porte-monnaie/*
in the cupboard. *ma clé/mon bébé dans l'armoire.*
How old is this bread? *De quand date ce pain?*
My bed sags/is hard/soft. *Mon lit est défoncé/trop dur/trop mou.*
The cold water is hot. *L'eau froide est chaude.*
I've scalded the baby. *J'ai échaudé le bébé.*
Call a doctor please. *Appelez un médicin s'il vous plaît.*
There is no plug for the *Il n'y a pas de bouchon pour*
basin/bath. *le lavabo/la baignoire.*
Please remove that spider. *Enlevez cette araignée, s'il vous plaît.*
Je vais faire la grasse matinée. I'm going to have a lie in.
J'en ai ras le bol. I'm fed up (with this).
J'en ai marre. I'm sick of this.
C'est marrant ça. That's funny (peculiar or ha! ha!)
Oh la vache! What a cow/Oh lord!/ How awful!
C'est vachement bien ça. That's really great.

Making the most of Paris

When you are in Museum Mood

Museum visits are made easy with the *Carte Musées et Monuments*, a pass valid in over 60 museums, worth buying if you are planning to make your visit intensely cultural. Available at museums, big Metro and RER stations and the Tourist Office, 127 avenue des Champs Élysées. Price: 1 day 80 Frs, 3 days 160 Frs, 5 days 240 Frs.

The **Louvre** is half price after 3pm, free the first Sunday in the month.

Queue-beating tip when the line at the pyramid looks like an overnight campout affair. **Arriving on foot**, stand facing the Tuileries with your back to the pyramid: to your left and right, next to the angels on pedestals, are stairwells leading to the underground entrance. **Arriving by metro**, get off at the Palais Royal-Musée du Louvre station and use the entrance signposted directly from the platform.

When you have Museum Indigestion

General tip: FUSAC (France-USA Contact) is a free, fortnightly magazine run mainly by and for the large and variegated American community in Paris but full of useful stuff for all on where to find community events, like-minded people, nannies, house-moving sales, etc. Can be found in the English-language bookshops and in bars, pubs, sandwich shops, in trendy areas.

1. Cinemas

Cinema programmes go from Wednesday to Tuesday: the week's listings are published on Wednesday mornings.

Information: Two publications, both in French, both cheap: *L'Officiel des Spectacles*, which costs the princely sum of 2 Frs (20p), and *Pariscope* which contains the same information plus film festival programmes and unsavoury advertisements for expensive telephone conversations and therefore costs 3 Frs (30p). Both carry information on theatres, exhibitions, concerts, cinemas, restaurants, nightclubs, etc.

Language: We all know that a disproportionate number of films were, and are, made in English so, if you want to see one of the latest productions or catch up on a golden oldie, lash out on a programme and plan a different kind of culture trip.
NB *Version originale* (*vo*) means 'original language' with French subtitles; *version française* (*vf*) means dubbed in French.

Which cinema? On any day of the year there are some 150 different films showing in the city and most central Paris cinemas systematically show films

Making the most of Paris

in their 'original language'. And there are a few cinemas that can be relied on to have good films in their undubbed versions. The majority of them are in the 5th and 6th arrondissements.

Examples: 5th arrondissement: Grand Action, Reflet Médicis, Espace St Michel, Studio Ursulines; 6th arrondissement: Action Christine, Racine, 3 Luxembourg. Also, near Montparnasse: Les 7 Parnassiens.

And there is one small, private 'chain' called MK2, owned by maverick distributor Marin Karmitz whose avowed aim is to remain independent from the big American cowboys and to promote good films rather than commercial blockbusters. A man to be encouraged.

Important - In some cases, you are still expected to tip the usherette - a modest 2 Frs or so will do. If this annoys you, just remember that this may be her only income.

2. Bookshops

All other things being equal, books are more expensive in France than in England, not because bookshops are greedier but because books carry a VAT rate of 19.6%.

English-Language Bookshops

Shakespeare & Co, 37 rue de la Bûcherie, Paris 5th.
Metro: Maubert-Mutualité.
This rambling old secondhand bookshop covers several floors with books stacked on the floor, squeezed into every staircase and more bookcases than walking space on the upper floors - irresistible. It is a long-standing Franco-American institution where Great Names We Have Nurtured - James Joyce in particular - are standard currency and the owner, George Whitman, still holds Sunday afternoon tea parties and poetry readings on the pavement. Mostly staffed by friendly American students.

WH Smith, 248 rue de Rivoli, Paris 1st. Metro: Concorde.
Yes, there is a Paris branch, refreshingly different and independent of the mother house, carrying a large number of books currently in print in Britain and America. Efficient, bilingual, mainly French staff.

Galignani, 224 rue de Rivoli, Paris 1st. Metro: Concorde.
"The first English bookshop on the Continent." A very smart Franco-Anglo-American bookshop with old-fashioned panelling and a superior atmosphere. Lots of art books, literature and browsing material as well as normal holiday books. Bilingual staff of both nationalities.

Making the most of Paris

Brentano's, 37 avenue de l'Opéra, Paris 2nd. Metro: Opéra.
Big American bookshop: endless corridors and corners with masses of
books, magazines, all kinds of upbeat stationery. A must for many - I once
saw a Rolls Royce + chauffeur park on the pavement and release two
fearfully smart, diminutive women who marched into the emporium of
culture with their enormous, gorilla-like bodyguard, all hands, at their
heels. The staff were just as friendly with him as they are with all clients.

Tea & Tattered Pages, 24 rue Mayet, Paris 6th. Metro: Duroc.
This is, as its name suggests, a tea-shop which also sells secondhand books.
A supremely friendly, student-like atmosphere in a small shop where people
come to read (even buy) books and sit chatting for hours.

Nouveau Quartier Latin (NQL), boulevard Saint Michel, Paris 6th.
One of the largest importers of foreign books, NQL stocks prescribed
university English course books and a good choice of general fiction,
poetry, drama and travel in English.

French Bookshops

A few are worth mentioning for their wide variety or narrow speciality.

FNAC The French answer to Smiths, Dillons, Waterstones and Menzies all
rolled into one. There are several branches in Paris (and in large provincial
towns), with big selections on all general subjects and usually an English-
language section -

Étoile	26 avenue des Ternes, Paris 17th.
Forum des Halles	1 rue Pierre Lescot, Paris 1st.
Saint Lazare	109 rue Saint Lazare, Paris 9th.
Montparnasse	136 rue de Rennes, Paris 6th.

Gibert Jeune	5 place Saint Michel, Paris 5th.
Joseph Gibert	26 boulevard Saint Michel, Paris 6th.

Facing each other and run by estranged members of the same family, they
are a sort of French Foyles who also sell stationery, records and secondhand
textbooks. Much frequented by the student population.

La Hune, 170 boulevard Saint Germain, Paris 6th.
A lively place just next to the Café de Flore, it stays open late in the evening
and has very good art and literature sections.

La Procure, 3 rue Mézières, Paris 6th.
Specialises in religion but has excellent philosophy and fiction sections too.
Much used by philosophy teachers and students.

Making the most of Paris

La Méridienne, 14 rue du Dragon, Paris 6th.
In a delightful courtyard, it sells books on therapy, spirituality and modern self-development.

La Maison du Dictionnaire, 98 boulevard du Montparnasse, Paris 14th.
Astounding! Nothing but dictionaries - languages, of course, even the most obscure; and all manner of technical, mechanical and electronical spheres.

3. Markets

Visit the food markets of Paris, soak up the feel of daily life here, even buy some of the ingredients that make it what it is. Covered markets may be in superb 19th-century iron-and-glass buildings. Some street markets consist of temporary stands set up two or three days a week, others are pedestrian streets where the permanent shops simply extend their space onto the pavements. They are always colourful, lively and full of temptations (plus a few pickpockets) among their amazingly-crafted mountains of fruit and vegetables. The stall-holders are unlikely to be locals - more probably from the suburbs, North Africa or Turkey, their styles in interesting contrast with those of their clients. The last half hour before closing time on Sundays - midday or 1pm - can be rich in unrefusable 'finishing up' offers.

But globalisation and standardisation threaten the more modest actors on this centuries-old stage. Brussels has ordered every cheese or meat van and stall to be refrigerated, something the smaller merchants simply cannot afford - several years' earnings for some - so the markets of France that we love because of their individuality, because they really are in touch with the earth, are heading for near-inevitable takeover by big concerns that centralise buying, reduce choice and bring the supermarket ethos to the canvas stall.

Covered Markets

Marché Saint Quentin, 10th, Metro: Gare de l'Est.
This magnificent 19th-century iron polygon has a wide variety of stalls including Portuguese, Italian and Kosher specialities, hardware and cobbling/keymaking shops as well as excellent cheese, vegetable, fish and charcuterie and a café in the middle!

Marché Saint Germain, 6th. Metro: Saint Germain des Prés.
Expensive but very good on fish and fresh vegetables. Also an excellent Greek stall with delicious picnic ingredients.

Making the most of Paris

Street Markets (every day except Mondays)

Place d'Aligre, 11th. Metro: Ledru-Rollin.
Cheapest of 'em all, but make sure of the quality before you buy. Tremendous atmosphere in the crush of eager shoppers, North African voices and spicy smells. The covered market has better stuff - at higher prices. Plus a tempting section dealing in junk, secondhand clothes and crockery on weekday mornings.

Rue Mouffetard, 5th. Metro: Monge.
Super little market at the bottom of the hill on place Saint Médard, and yet more tempting stands, shops and eating places as you walk up towards the Place de la Contrescarpe and the historic centre of the Latin Quarter.

Rue de Buci, 6th. Metro: Odéon.
This is smart Saint Germain des Prés so don't expect great bargains. But a street strewn with banana skins and cabbage leaves will automatically have a relaxed, natural air to it, however Great and Good the individuals lining up for their apple a day. And one or two nice pavement cafés.

Rue Montorgueil, 2nd. Metro: Étienne Marcel.
The ghostly remnants of the old central market, Les Halles (*le ventre de Paris* - the belly of Paris), that was moved out of the city centre in the 70s. The atmosphere is less earthy than in the old days but the pedestrian area is alive and busy and fun to stroll through.

Rue Cler, 7th. Metro: Latour Maubourg.
Nicely crowded and bustly and human in a fairly smart, superior neighbourhood.

Rue de Lévis, 17th. Metro: Villiers.
Again, in an area of smart buildings with well-heeled occupants, a car-empty, market-filled street where people take time to pick and choose and to talk to each other.

Occasional Street Markets

Open mornings only (8am-1pm), they are often cheaper and simpler than the daily markets. The best are probably:

Boulevard de Port-Royal, Paris 5th. Metro: Gobelins.
Tuesday, Thursday, Saturday.

Boulevard Auguste Blanqui, Paris 13th. Metro: Corvisart.
Tuesday, Friday, Saturday.

Boulevard Edgar Quinet, Paris 14th. Metro: Edgar Quinet.
Wednesday, Saturday.

Making the most of Paris

Boulevard Richard Lenoir, Paris 11th. Metro: Bastille.
Thursday, Sunday.

Organic

And, although most of the others have one organic/health-food stall, there are two wholly organic weekly markets (*marchés biologiques*) that are worth a visit if you care about natural food, soap, cosmetics, etc.

Saturday mornings: **Boulevard des Batignolles, Paris 17th. Metro: Rome.**
Sunday mornings: **Boulevard Raspail, Paris 6th. Metro: Sèvres-Babylone.**

Fabrics

Cleaning ladies and countesses will go all the way to Montmartre to buy the fabrics and accessories they need for their dressmaking or interior decoration projects. The Marché Saint Pierre, a series of shops in the little streets at the bottom of the Square Willette which itself sits beneath the Sacré Coeur, is a Parisian institution. Here, especially at the house of Dreyfus, they know they will find a wide choice of reasonably-priced materials (the wealthy Dreyfus family are more likely to be found frequenting their countess clients than their cleaning ladies).

Stamps and phonecards

There has been a stamp collectors' exchange market on the pavement benches on Avenue Matignon, just off the Rond-Point des Champs Élysées, for years. It has kept up with the times and now deals in phonecards as well. All day Thursday, Saturday, Sunday.

4. Gardens

The public 'green spaces' (*espaces verts*) of Paris are few and far between, which makes them all the more precious. Most are rather formally French with a small piece called *le jardin anglais* where things are meant to look more spontaneous and 'wild' - the 'English' look. More and more municipal gardeners are sowing tough grass seed so that, at last, the French may be allowed to walk and sit on the grass in their public gardens; a few still hold dear the old interdiction and employ whistlers to keep order. Paris gardens are ALL full of people at weekends.

Visits

Paris City Hall organises excellent guided visits of Paris parks and gardens: see page 171 for details.

Fête des Jardins On one weekend a year, over 100 gardens, large and small, that are otherwise closed to the public are visible - the difficulty is choosing which ones to visit in the short space of time. 3rd weekend in September.

Making the most of Paris

On the edge

The two biggest 'green areas' are outside the boundaries of Paris proper: the Bois de Boulogne on the western front, the Bois de Vincennes to the east. Both have lakes where you can go rowing, both have roads through them but still manage to grow more trees and grass than the rest of Paris's parks put together. Boulogne, definitely the smarter of the two, has a couple of famous race courses (Longchamp and Auteuil) and an 'amusement park' - the Jardin d'Acclimatation - a deliciously old-fashioned hangover from gentler days where contemporary French children still seem happy with swings and slides and the little zoo. Vincennes, which also has a race course, is more of a people's park and has a wonderful old 17th-century fort.

Inside the walls (Paris intramuros = the 20 arrondissements)

Inside Paris, the Luxembourg garden is still a favourite with the solid old Senate building (Palais du Luxembourg) as its backdrop. There is enormous character in its extraordinarily declarative 19th-century statues, studied French formality and very staid, definitely pre-90s amusements for children. They come in the form of really slow pony rides and model-yacht-sailing on the pond (boats for hire on the spot - NO motors). The old *chaisières* - chair ladies - tyrants who used to come round demanding a few centimes for the chair you had chosen to sit on, have gone; but the population is still an interesting mixture of Left Bank *grand-mères* and Sorbonne students.

The next slot goes to the newest garden in Paris, the **Parc André Citroën**, way down the river beyond the Eiffel Tower. Built on the site of the old car factories, it is a brilliant study in modern landscaping and theming for a public park. It has two very daring greenhouses and several smaller ones, all built with what look like smoothed-down tree trunks, a series of colour gardens, some fascinating waterworks and a balanced mix of open space and secluded corners. They have even created an overgrown, weedy, 'bomb-site' area. Well worth the trip.

Leading back from the Eiffel Tower, the **Champ de Mars** was laid out at the end of the 18th century as the practice ground for manoeuvres by students at the École Militaire: it has some nice spots with benches (and uniformed females with whistles to shoo you off the grass). Out in the 19th arrondissement, the magnificent **Buttes Chaumont** (*monts chauves* or bald hills) is a series of steep hills (windmills used to stand here) and a reproduction of the Sibyl's Temple - deliciously 19th century.

Two less well-known parks: the **Parc Montsouris**, on the southern edge of Paris, is hilly and green and natural-looking and, in the smart residential

Making the most of Paris

neighbourhood north of the Champs Elysées, the **Parc Monceau** (another bald hill) still has the highly aristocratic bearing of its origins (it was built in 1780 as the private garden, then twice as big, for the Duke of Chartres' country cottage).

And there are hidden green treasures behind high walls, inside ministry buildings, in hospital grounds. Not all are open to the public, of course, but you risk no more than a stiff watchdog's bark if you stick your nose in where you're not wanted, so do try. The gardens of the **Hôpital La Pitié/Salpêtrière** are a wonderful surprise - and the hospital chapel is almost the size of a small cathedral. The **Hôpital Saint Louis** has unexpected peace round the lawns and flowerbeds of its ancient courtyards. Built at the same time, in the same style and by the same architect as the brick-and-stone Place des Vosges, it is also an architectural curiosity (there's a lot of modern hospital in the grounds now, too, of course). The garden of the **Rodin Museum** (accessible if you buy a museum ticket) makes a visit there even more rewarding and the **Palais Royal** enfolds a delightful leafy and airy space within its stone embrace. In the **Square Catherine Laboure** (Rue de Babylone) is a real and beautifully-kept kitchen garden while on the roof of the Gare Montparnasse is a huge surprise: the **Jardin Atlantique**, a diminutive 'park' with trees, paths, corners and vistas.

Les Serres d'Auteuil, 3 avenue de la Porte d'Auteuil, 16th. Metro: Porte d'Auteuil.
Owned by the city, those lovely 19th-century glasshouses are really worth a visit. They still grow seedlings for the public parks and gardens, though the palm trees and Japanese carp just live their lives out here.

Last, as in every great city, the cemeteries (*cimetières*) are places of vegetation, stone and eternal rest and some people enjoy the search for memorials to Great Heroes (or pop singers, or politicians). **Montparnasse** on the Left Bank, **Père Lachaise** on the Right Bank are the best known but **Montmartre** also has some interesting tombs on its hillside.

How to get there

Jardin d'Acclimatation/Bois de Boulogne Metro: Porte Maillot, Sablons.
Bois de Vincennes Metro: Château de Vincennes.
Jardin du Luxembourg Metro: Odéon.
Champ de Mars Metro: École Militaire.
Buttes Chaumont Metro: Buttes Chaumont.
Parc Montsouris Metro: Cité Universitaire.
Parc Monceau Metro: Monceau.
Hôpital La Pitié/Salpêtrière Metro: St Marcel.

Making the most of Paris

Hôpital St Louis Metro: Goncourt.
Musée Rodin Metro: Varenne.
Palais Royal Metro: Palais Royal.
Cimetière Montparnasse Metro: Edgar Quinet.
Cimetière Père Lachaise Metro: Père Lachaise.
Cimetière de Montmartre Metro: Place de Clichy.

5. Walks

The River Seine obviously serves as the city's largest lung but walking along the riverside was made difficult in the 1990s because the authorities believed they had to offer as much space as possible to King Car. Ideas are changing and some of those fume-filled riverside ways are being returned to the humble pedestrian and his dog.

The plan is to provide unbroken pathways and footbridges from the Parc de Bercy in the east right round to the Parc André Citroën in the west - a 12-kilometre dream of which a chunk in the east has already come true.

The two islands Cité and Saint Louis are good wandering areas too, apart from the main north-south drag between Châtelet and Saint Michel. Guided walks, in French or English, are listed every week in the What's On programmes - *L'Officiel des Spectacles* and *Pariscope*. Here are a very few suggestions from us.

5.1 See the permanent open-air sculpture garden along the river west of the **Gare d'Austerlitz** below the Quai Saint Bernard. At the end, cross over to **Ile Saint Louis** and walk along by those elegant 17th-century apartment buildings, built for the high-born and wealthy of their day and still very select places to live. Take the **Pont Saint Louis** across to the **Ile de la Cité** and the little garden below the east end of **Notre Dame** - don't miss the memorial to the Jewish deportees at the very eastern point of the garden.

Walk west along the cathedral, gazing up at the stone miracles overhead, across the square past the hospital that is still known by its medieval name of God's Hostel (**Hôtel Dieu**) and right for a brief spell in all that traffic until you reach the **Flower Market** which feels like a slice of tropical jungle lost - and found - in northern Europe. And here is the Cité metro station with its original Guimard entrance, whence you can go north or south as you wish.

5.2 As well as its world-famous examples of national building styles, built between the '20s and the '50s to house foreign and French students in an ideal of harmony and international understanding, the **Cité Universitaire** is in fact a vast 40-hectare park, so visitors can combine culture AND fresh(er) air.

Making the most of Paris

5.3 The deliciously immobile, old-fashioned **Canal Saint Martin** which forms a wandering perpendicular to the Seine from Quai de la Rapée (one stretch is in a tunnel) was condemned to death by concrete in the 1970s, to make a road, of course, but good sense prevailed. It is a stretch of tree-lined water where pleasure barges climb up and down the nine locks, Sunday afternoons are no-traffic times on the roads alongside and walking northwards is most enjoyable, ending with the treat of a good MK2 cinema and café on the banks of the **Bassin de la Villette**. Canal trips inside Paris or out into the countryside along the River Marne or the Canal de l'Ourcq are organised by Canauxrama, based at Bassin de la Villette.

5.4 A walkway has been built on the old overhead railway line between Bastille (just SE of) and Daumesnil. Called the *Coulée Verte* (the Green Stream), it is effectively a long thin garden that has been equipped with trees and bushes, benches and entrance staircases and runs all the way at 2nd-floor level above the road. A most original addition to the grass-starved Paris scene and when you have had enough of walking in a straight line you can take the stairs down and visit the craftsmen working (and exhibiting and selling their wares) underneath the arches.

6. High Places

Apart from the inevitable **Eiffel Tower** (the highest spot at 276 metres but it costs a lot to get to the top), you can climb the steps to the top of the towers of **Notre Dame** (69m) for an incomparable view over the heart of medieval Paris and a study of the architecture of the cathedral itself. The department store **La Samaritaine**, at Châtelet, has lifts to its top floor, a café on the roof terrace and charges nothing for this bird's-eye view of the very centre of Paris (46m). The **Tour Montparnasse** is the second highest viewing point (209m) and has "the fastest lifts in Europe" to its 52nd floor (about 50 Frs; open for night-time visits).

7. Cookery demonstrations are given by Cordon Bleu every weekday

morning. They last 2-3 hours, are given or translated into English and end with a tasting. Price 220 Frs. Book 48hrs ahead on tel. 01 53 68 22 50.

8. Getting around Paris

How Paris is designed. Finding your way in Paris is made easier if you know that -

1. The city is divided into 20 arrondissements laid out in a clockwise spiral pattern that starts at Place de la Concorde.

2. Street numbering is based on the Seine, i.e. streets perpendicular to the river are numbered outwards from it, odds on the left, evens on the

Making the most of Paris

right; streets parallel to the river are numbered as the river flows, east to west.

3. The Left Bank is the south bank, the Right Bank is the north bank of the River Seine.

The maps in this guide are not street maps. Bring or buy one of the Indispensable™, Taride™, Michelin or other pocket street atlases and get the excellent map of metro and buslines free from any metro station.

Don't use your car. It will cost you a fortune in parking (or police pound) fees and take years off your life in frustration before you find that parking spot. Also, Paris is already dangerously polluted and no-one needs to add to that.

Do use the wonderful public transport system, run by the RATP. It is one of the best in the world. Some bus routes are perfect tours of Paris and its monuments.

Buses

The No **24** crosses the Seine twice and runs along the south embankment between the bridges. Other good routes are **30**, **48**, **73**, **82** and **90**. Left-bank route **88**, the first new bus line in 50 years, opened in 1998 between the Cité Universitaire and the Parc André Citroën, takes you past Montparnasse and the exciting new architecture of the Place de Catalogne, then on through the residential 15th arrondissement to the high-rise buildings of the new Left Bank development called Front de Seine.

Metro

You are never far from one of the 300-odd metro stations and trains that run between 5.30am and about 1am. Many of the stations have been radically refurbished in the last few years, especially for the metro's 100th anniversary in 2000, and are full of interest just for themselves. The brand new line 14 is a showcase for the latest thing in driverless trains - far more staff presence actually on the platforms - and is designed to take some of the load off the other Right-Bank lines between the great new Bibliothèque François Mitterand and the Madeleine.

Tickets

Fares are paid according to the number of zones crossed. Visitors will normally not go outside zones 1 and 2, the city limits.

One ticket is valid for one journey by bus, metro or RER within zones 1 and 2.

You should keep your ticket for inspection at any time and for the **turnstiles** out of RER systems.

Making the most of Paris

Single tickets cost 8 Frs*, a book of 10 tickets costs 58 Frs.
A one-day ticket for two zones - *Mobilis* - costs 32 Frs.
A two-zone pass - *Carte Orange* - for unlimited travel by the holder
(passport photo required) within the two zones for one week: 85 Frs per
person; for one month: 285 Frs per person.

Other formulas for one to five days exist to cover more zones (*Paris Visite*)
or to include museum entrance (*Carte Musée*).

* Prices valid at time of going to press.

Batobus

Not the speediest way to travel but great fun with lots to see, the boatbus
uses the great watery road through the middle of Paris to take you, in six
stops, from the Eiffel Tower to the Hôtel de Ville.

Bicycles

You can hire a bike and launch yourself bravely into the scrum alone or you
can take a guided bike tour, in French or English, from

Paris-Vélo, 2 rue du Fer-à-Moulin, 5th. Tel: 01 43 37 59 22.

**Paris à Vélo c'est Sympa, 37 boulevard Bourdon, 4th.
Tel: 01 48 87 60 01**, have bikes for hire - folding bikes, tandems, baby
seats. Their mouthful of a name translates roughly as 'Paris by Bike is
Great'.

Roller Skates and Roller Blades

If you want a direct experience of what lively outdoor Paris is doing today,
go to **Nomades, 37 boulevard Bourdon, 4th. Tel: 01 44 54 07 44.**
The relaxed occupants will offer you a raft of entertainments:

• Roller skates and blades for hire at 50-60 Frs per day, 10 Frs for the
  armour-plating.

• The latest in rollers for you to test at 100 Frs per day.

• Lessons on their indoor roller-floor then outside on the pavement.

• Sunday afternoon roller-treks from their front door. These draw
  hundreds, even thousands, of enthusiasts and are free (once you have
  hired your wheels, of course).

• On Saturday evenings, role-play sessions upstairs - costumes and effects
  of all sorts. All-night sessions once a month.

• At other times, space for card games, board games, hanging out. I felt the
  place had a really good atmosphere. (It has council backing.)

Making the most of Paris

Roller Station, 107 boulevard Beaumarchais, 3rd,
Tel: 01 42 78 33 00, also hire out roller skates and blades.

Airport Buses

Orlybus between Orly Airport and Place Denfert-Rochereau, Paris 14th.
Roissybus between Charles-de-Gaulle Airport and Opéra, Paris 9th.
Air France buses between: Charles-de-Gaulle Airport and Étoile or Porte Maillot or Montparnasse; Orly Airport and Invalides or Montparnasse.
Airport Shuttle is a private door-to-door minibus service at very reasonable prices. Some hotels subscribe to the service. Otherwise, the telephone is 01 45 38 55 72.

Petrol round the clock

Antar, 42 rue Beaubourg, 1st. Esso, 338 rue Saint Honoré, 1st.
Total, parking George V, 8th.
168 rue du Faubourg Saint Martin, 10th.
7/11 boulevard Garibaldi, 15th.

Dates to remember

Late Feb-early March: Salon de l'Agriculture
Porte de Versailles, 15th. Metro: Porte de Versailles.
When the countryside comes to the capital, bringing with it "the biggest farm in Europe", its finest bulls, ewes and carrots, in a joyous atmosphere of Crufts-for-Cows plus Giant-Pumpkin-Competition; also some wonderful opportunities to sample fine regional cooking.

Mid-March: Le Printemps des Rues
Between République, Bastille and Nation, performances by hundreds of street entertainers.

April-May: La Foire du Trône
Pelouse de Reuilly, 12th. Metro: Porte Dorée.
A gigantic funfair where the families and youth of Paris and the suburbs flock for ghost trains, roundabouts and candyfloss.

Good Friday: Le Chemin de Croix
Montmartre: Square Willette, 18th. Metro: Anvers.
The Archbishop of Paris goes through the stations of the cross on the way up to the Sacré Cœur.

End June: La Course des Garçons de Café
A supremely Parisian race, this, where several hundred café waiters and waitresses in full regalia - black suit, white apron, glass-laden tray - run a

Making the most of Paris

crazy distance (those who finish cover 5 miles) along the boulevards, with those glasses on that tray.

13 & 14 July: Bastille Day
The famous *bals populaires* (street dancing) are on the evening before the day itself. Parisians dance at Place de la Bastille, of course, and also at Fire Stations: the *bals des pompiers* are famous. The 14th is the official day: military parade on the Champs Élysées in the morning, city fireworks over the Trocadéro in the evening.

3rd weekend in September: Fête des Jardins
All over town.
The Paris Gardens Festival is a short opportunity to discover some of the secret greenery of this all-stone city. Programme from the Tourist Office or one of the Mairies (cf. Gardens p.147).

1st weekend October: Montmartre wine harvest
More festivities than litres of wine: the event is lots bigger than the harvest from this tiny vineyard but it is full of fun and pseudo-traditional ritual. The wine, pressed in the Mairie itself, is expensive for what it is... before that exclusive label goes on.

2nd week November: Marjolaine - Green Lifestyle exhibition
Parc Floral de Paris, Bois de Vincennes, 12th. Metro: Château de Vincennes.
Stands and stalls, lectures and lessons - everyone in the green, organic, environmental or alternative health world comes to see and be seen; new and interesting products and ideas are launched here every year.

Winter (December-March): Hôtel de Ville Skating Rink (Patinoire)
Free skating for all on the City Council's open-air ice rink beside the 'wedding-cake' City Hall - bring your own skates or hire on the spot. A surprising and unusual atmosphere of friendly sharing in an enclosed space in the very centre of Paris.

An Introduction to French period furniture

To enliven your reading of the entries in this book and perhaps illumine your stay in the hotels listed, here is a very brief history of French furniture in the 17th, 18th and 19th centuries with the essential features of each style, an illustration by Mathias Fournier and the dates of the king or government associated with the name (the period often covers more time than the actual reign).

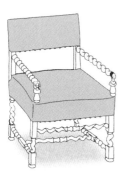

Louis XIII 1610-1643

Solid, square and massive are the key characteristics here. Twists and turns, carvings and heavy ornamentation with 'grotesque' masks, figurines and cherubs, garlands, bunches of fruit and scrollwork to decorate the dark wood of the structure.

Louis XIV 1643-1715

Louis was five when he came to the throne and reigned in person from 1661. Luxurious and elaborate describe his period and Boulle, founder of his own style and first in a line of craftsmen, was the leading designer and cabinet-maker. He launched the fashion for using expensive foreign woods plus tortoishell, ivory and brass as inlay; gilt bronze for corner trim, handles and finger-plate decoration; deeply carved garlands, festoons, allegorical motifs and mythological figures to celebrate the power and wealth of the régime, elaborate curves to counteract the solid squareness of earlier times.

An Introduction to French period furniture

Régence 1715-1723*

Reaction to the excesses of Louis' court lifestyle set in before he died. The need was for quieter, more informal surroundings. Furniture became lighter, less elaborately adorned, more gently shaped. Heavy, deepset carvings and bronze bits were replaced by flat curves and flowing ribbons. Life, manners and art became less declamatory, less pompous, more delicate.

*Almost a century before the English Regency period.

Louis XV 1715-1771

Another child king, he reigned in person after 1723. The Régence search for more delicacy led, under Louis XV, into the Rococo style and the craze for all things oriental - Chinoiserie was IN with its lacquer, ivory and mother-of-pearl inlays and lively, exotic scenes of faraway places. Comfort was important too, with fine fabrics and well-padded chairs. So was beautiful handiwork: the period produced some superb craftsmen.

An Introduction to French period furniture

Louis XVI 1774-1793

Instantly recognisable by its tapering fluted legs and straight lines, this is the style associated with Marie-Antoinette and the yearning of sophisticated urbanites for a simpler Golden Age when the countryside was the source of all Good, though few actually made the transition. Furniture was often painted in 'rustic' pastel colours, and marquetry was still widely used for more formal pieces. The simplicity of classical forms was the model, inspired by numerous archaeological expeditions.

Directoire 1795-1799

This is when women started to dress like Greek goddesses and gentlemen wore long flowing coats and high boots. Furniture design continued the trend towards simple flowing lines, less decoration and ever more reference to ancient Rome (Pompeii revealed its treasure at this time, to everyone's great excitement).

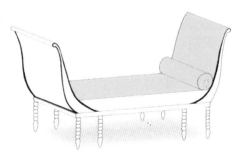

An Introduction to French period furniture

Empire 1704-1815

The Emperor was Napoleon I, the inspiration was his booty from the Egyptian campaigns - as well as more Ancient Greece and Rome. Ormolu ornamentation took the form of sphinxes' busts, winged lions and forms were even direct copies from Antiquity. Later, the trend was to over-elaboration and a certain type of decadence.

Fauteuil Voltaire 1850s

With or without arms, usually dressed in tapestry-style weave or deep-coloured plush and shiny studs, this is a ubiquitous item in French houses, hotels and inns. Voltaire, philosopher of religious, political and social liberty and recognised figurehead of the 18th-century Enlightenment, died in 1778. His portraits often show him wearing a soft velvety coat and floppy lace trimmings. The chair that bears his name is in fact a mid-19th-century invention but it matches the popular image of Voltaire and one can well imagine the great man reclining in his lace cuffs and addressing a group of literary ladies in a smart salon.

French furniture

Napoleon III 1852-1870

This period, also known as Second Empire, just to confuse you, or the Beaux-Arts style, was the French equivalent of heavy Victorian. Thick velvet drapes hung everywhere, tassels, swags, fringes adorned them, keeping the light out; the classical style became massive and was decorated with pints of gilding; it used rich dark colours, heavy dark woods, much gilt bronze ornamentation (e.g. little balconies round little occasional tables, elaborate light fittings), veined marble tops on storage pieces.

Quick reference indices

WHEELCHAIR

Places with facilities for people in wheelchairs but please check for your specific requirements when booking.

- 18 Le Clos Médicis
- 27 Daguerre
- 48 La Villa
- 57 Orsay
- 65 Bosquet-Tour Eiffel
- 67 Tulipe
- 69 Frémiet
- 71 Hameau de Passy
- 83 Régence Étoile
- 87 Flaubert
- 94 Lavoisier
- 97 Favart
- 99 Pulitzer

GARDEN - PATIO

These places have gardens or patios where guests can sit.

- 8 Gilden Magenta
- 10 St Paul le Marais
- 13 Le Jeu de Paume
- 18 Le Clos Médicis
- 25 Les Gobelins
- 42 Aubusson
- 43 Nesle
- 44 L'Hôtel
- 45 Millésime
- 46 Hôtel des Marronniers
- 49 Danube
- 59 Varenne
- 63 Eiffel Park
- 67 Tulipe
- 71 Hameau de Passy
- 73 Massenet
- 81 Résidence Impériale
- 82 Centre Ville Étoile
- 87 Flaubert
- 92 Jardin de Villiers

MODEM

Hotels where guests can connect into a modem socket or a phone socket in their bedrooms. If Internet access is important to you, we do advise you to bring your own adapter for French telephone sockets, though most places will have one adapter available at reception.

- 1 Brighton
- 4 Relais du Louvre
- 6 Britannique
- 10 St Paul le Marais
- 11 7è Art
- 13 Le Jeu de Paume
- 18 Le Clos Médicis
- 22 Minerve
- 24 St Christophe
- 25 Les Gobelins
- 32 Le Sainte Beuve
- 33 Le Saint Grégoire
- 34 Ferrandi
- 35 Balcons
- 38 Odéon
- 42 Aubusson
- 44 L'Hôtel
- 45 Millésime
- 48 La Villa
- 50 Le Madison
- 52 Lenox St Germain
- 53 Université
- 54 Verneuil
- 55 Lille
- 57 Orsay
- 58 Bourgogne & Montana
- 61 Bailli de Suffren
- 62 Le Tourville
- 64 Lévêque
- 65 Relais Bosquet-Tour Eiffel
- 74 Jardins du Trocadéro
- 75 Kléber
- 76 Franklin Roosevelt
- 77 L'Elysée
- 80 Pergolèse
- 81 Résidence Impériale

Quick reference indices

- 84 Étoile Park
- 85 Princesse Caroline
- 87 Flaubert
- 88 Eber Monceau
- 90 Banville
- 91 Neuville
- 92 Jardin de Villiers
- 94 Le Lavoisier
- 95 Newton Opéra
- 99 Pulitzer Opéra
- 102 Prima Lepic

ARCHITECTURE & DESIGN

Places with particularly striking architectural or design features.

Old architecture and styles:
17th - 19th centuries

- 1 Brighton
- 7 Saint Merry
- 9 Bretonnerie
- 13 Le Jeu de Paume
- 32 Louis II
- 37 Globe
- 42 Aubusson
- 44 L'Hôtel
- 53 Université
- 58 Bourgogne & Montana
- 69 Frémiet
- 74 Jardins du Trocadéro
- 77 L'Elysée
- 96 Croisés
- 100 Villa Fénelon

20th-century architecture

- 30 Raspail Montparnasse
- 78 Elysées Matignon
- 82 Centre Ville

INTERIOR DESIGN

Traditional and contemporary

- 11 7è Art
- 43 Nesle
- L'Hôtel
- 48 La Villa
- 50 Le Madison
- 52 Lenox St Germain
- 54 Verneuil
- 57 Orsay
- 58 Bourgogne & Montana
- 72 Nicolo
- 80 Pergolèse
- 90 Banville
- 93 New Orient
- 94 Lavoisier
- 99 Pulitzer Opéra

A short history of the Company

Perhaps the best clue as to why these books have their own very particular style and 'bent' lies in Alastair's history.

After a law degree, a stint as a teacher in Voluntary Service Overseas led to a change in direction. He became a teacher (French and Spanish) and then a refugee worker, then spent several years in overseas development work before settling into environmental campaigning, and even green politics. Meanwhile, he was able to dabble - just once a year - in an old interest, taking clients on tours of special places all over Europe. This grew, eventually, into a travel company (it still exists as Alastair Sawday's Tours, operating, inter alia, walking and biking tours all over Europe).

Trying to take his clients to eat and sleep in places that were not owned by corporations and assorted bandits he found dozens of very special places in France - farms, châteaux etc - a list that grew into the first book, French Bed and Breakfast. It was a celebration of 'real' places to stay and the remarkable people who run them.

So, this publishing company is based on the success of that first and rather whimsical French book. It started as mild crusade, and there it stays. For we still celebrate the unusual, the beautiful, the highly individual. We have no rules for owners; they do things their own way. We are passionate about rejecting the ugly, the cold, the banal and the indifferent. And we are still passionate about promoting the use of 'real' food. Alastair is a trustee of the Soil Association and keen to promote organic growing especially.

It is a source of huge pleasure to us that we seem to have pressed the right button: there are thousands and thousands of people who, clearly, share our views and take up our ideas. We are by no means alone in trumpeting the virtues of standing up to the monstrous uniformity of so much of our culture.

The greatest accolade we have had was in The Bookseller magazine, which described us as 'head and shoulders above the rest'. That meant a lot. But even more satisfying is that we are building a company in which people matter. We are delighted to hear of new friendships between those in the book and those using it and to know that there are many people - among them artists, farmers, champions of the countryside - who have been enabled to pursue their unusual lives thanks to the extra income the book brings them.

Of course we want the company to flourish, but this isn't just about money; it is about people, too.

Vivement les vacances
Roll on the holidays

Après ça, il nous faudrait juste une petite chambre
pour deux Rive Gauche
After that, all we need is a little room for two on the Left Bank

Alastair Sawday
Special Places to Stay series

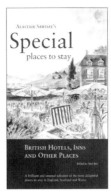

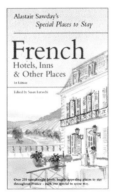

Tel: 01275 464891
Fax: 01275 464887
www.sawdays.co.uk

The Little Earth Book

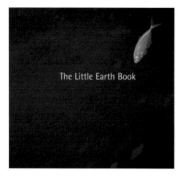

The Little Earth Book

Alastair Sawday, the publisher of this (wonderful) guidebook, is also an environmentalist. For over 25 years he has campaigned, not only against the worst excesses of modern tourism and its hotels, but against environmental 'looniness' of other kinds. He has fought for systems and policies that might enable our beautiful planet - simply - to survive. He founded and ran Avon Friends of the Earth, has run for Parliament, and has led numerous local campaigns. He is now a trustee of the Soil Association, experience upon which he draws in this remarkable new book.

Researched and written by an eminent Bristol architect, James Bruges, *The Little Earth Book* is a clarion call to action, a mind-boggling collection of mini-essays on today's most important environmental concerns, from global warming and poisoned food to economic growth, Third World debt, genes and 'superbugs'. Undogmatic but sure-footed, the style is light, explaining complex issues with easy language, illustrations and cartoons. Ideas are developed chapter by chapter, yet each one stands alone. It is an easy browse.

The Little Earth Book provides hope, with new ideas and examples of people swimming against the current, of bold ideas that work in practice.
It is a book as important as it is original. One has been sent to every M.P. Now you, too, can learn about the issues and join the most important debate of this century.

Oh - one last thing: *The Little Earth Book* is a damned good read! Note what Jonathon Porritt says about it:

"The Little Earth Book is different. And instructive. And even fun."

Did you know.....

- If everyone adopted the Western lifestyle we would need five earths to support us

- 60% of infections picked up in hospitals are now drug-resistant

- Environmental disasters have already created 80 MILLION refugees.

Order Form UK

All these books are available in major bookshops or you may order them direct. Post and packaging are FREE.

	Price	No. copies
Special Places to Stay: **Portugal**		
Edition 1	£8.95	
Special Places to Stay: **Spain**		
Edition 4	£11.95	
Special Places to Stay: **Ireland**		
Edition 3	£10.95	
Special Places to Stay: **Paris Hotels**		
Edition 3	£8.95	
Special Places to Stay: **Garden Bed & Breakfast**		
Edition 1	£10.95	
Special Places to Stay: **French Bed & Breakfast**		
Edition 6	£13.95	
Special Places to Stay: **British Hotels, Inns** and other places		
Edition 2	£10.95	
Special Places to Stay: **British Bed & Breakfast**		
Edition 5	£12.95	
Special Places to Stay: **French Hotels, Inns** and other places		
Edition 1	£11.95	
Special Places to Stay: **Italy** (from Rome to the Alps)		
Edition 1	£9.95	
The Little Earth Book	£4.99	

Please make cheques payable to: **Alastair Sawday Publishing**   **Total** [ ]

Please send cheques to: Alastair Sawday Publishing, The Home Farm, Barrow Gurney, Bristol BS48 3RW. **For credit card orders call 01275 464891 or order directly from our website www.sawdays.co.uk**

Name:

Address:

Postcode:

Tel: Fax:

If you do not wish to receive mail from other companies, please tick the box ❏   PH3

Order Form USA

All these books are available at your local bookstore, or you may order direct. Allow two to three weeks for delivery.

Special Places to Stay: **British Hotels, Inns** and other places   Price   No. copies

Edition 2	$17.95	

Special Places to Stay: **British Bed & Breakfast**

Edition 5	$19.95	

Special Places to Stay: **French Hotels, Inns** and other places

Edition 1	$19.95	

Special Places to Stay: **French Bed & Breakfast**

Edition 6	$19.95	

Special Places to Stay: **Garden Bed & Breakfast**

Edition 1	$17.95	

Special Places to Stay in Ireland

Edition 3	$17.95	

Special Places to Stay in Spain & Portugal

Edition 3	$19.95	

Special Places to Stay: **Italy (from Rome to the Alps)**

Edition 1	$14.95	

Shipping in the continental USA: $3.95 for one book, $4.95 for two books, $5.95 for three or more books. Outside continental USA, call (800) 243-0495 for prices. For delivery to AK, CA, CO, CT, FL, GA, IL, IN, KS, MI, MN, MO, NE, NM, NC, OK, SC, TN, TX, VA, and WA, please add appropriate sales tax

Please make checks payable to: The Globe Pequot Press   Total

To order by phone with MasterCard or Visa: (800) 243-0495. 9 a.m. to 5 p.m. EST; by fax: (800) 820-2329, 24 hours; through our Website: www.globe-pequot.com; or by mail: The Globe Pequot Press, P.O. Box 480, Guilford, CT 06437.

Name: Date:

Address:

Town:

State: Zip code:

Tel: Fax:

Report Form

Comments on existing entries and new discoveries.

If you have any comments on entries in this guide, please let us have them. If you have a favourite house, hotel, inn or other new discovery, please let us know about it.

Report on:

Entry no: _____ Edition: _____

New recommendation: _____

Name of property: _____

Address: _____

_____ Postcode: _____

Tel: _____

Comments: _____

_____

_____

_____

_____

_____

_____

_____

_____

From: _____

Address: _____

_____ Postcode: _____

Tel: _____

Please send the completed form to: **Alastair Sawday Publishing, The Home Farm, Barrow Gurney, Bristol BS48 3RW, UK**

Thank you.

Booking form - Bulletin de Réservation
Paris Hotels

À l'attention de:
To:
_____

Date:
_____

Madame, Monsieur

Veuillez faire la réservation suivante au nome de:
Please make the following booking for (name):
_____

Pour	*nuit(s)*	*Arrivant le:*	*jour*	*mois*	*année*
For	night(s)	Arriving:	day	month	year
		Départ le:	*jour*	*mois*	*année*
		Leaving:	day	month	year

Si possible, nous aimerions   *chambres, disposées comme suit:*
We would like   rooms, arranged as follows:

À grand lit   *À lits jumeaux*
Double bed   Twin beds

Pour trois   *À un lit simple*
Triple   Single

Suite   *Appartement*
Suite   Apartment

Veuillez nous envoyer la confirmation à l'adresse ci-dessous:
Please send confirmation to the following address:

Nom: Name:
_____

Adresse: Address:
_____
_____
_____

Tel No: E-mail:
_____

Fax No:
_____

Paris gardens visits in English

A very special experience

In June, July, August and September, the City of Paris Gardens Department organises guided visits in English, at 38 Frs per person (2001 price), of:

Parc André Citroën, Paris 15th.

An exceptional contemporary creation beside the Seine with a fantastic choice of plants in all kinds of atmospheres - wide lawns, little secret corners, enormous water features, a giant greenhouse - where the natural contrasts strikingly with the carefully constructed.

Visit on Saturdays at 10.30am.
Meet at entrance to Jardin Noir, corner of Rue Balard and Rue St Charles (Metro: Balard).

Parc de Bercy, Paris 12th.

Newly built on the site of the wine market, on the bank of the Seine opposite the new National Library, it has a delightful kitchen garden, a scented rose garden, a vast lawn, tall old trees and a deliciously romantic area, a riot of colour in summer.

Visit on Tuesdays at 3pm.
Meet inside the park, on the lawn opposite the former American Cultural Centre (from Metro Bercy, take Rue de Bercy to No 51).

Père Lachaise cemetery, Paris 20th.

Come for a comtemplative stroll through this shady 200-year-old cemetery, a veritable open-air sculpture gallery, past the graves of such famous names as Delacroix, Oscar Wilde, Gertrude Stein, Chopin, Jim Morrison, Balzac, Simone Signoret.

Visit on Saturdays at 3pm.
Meet at main entrance on Boulevard de Ménilmontant (Metro: Père Lachaise or Philippe Auguste).

The department also offers guided visits in French of 120 different gardens all year round. Tel: (0)1 40 71 75 60.

Index

Index

Index

Exchange rate table

French FF	Euro	US $	£ Sterling
10	1.52	1.29	0.91
50	7.60	6.45	4.55
100	15.20	12.90	9.10
150	22.80	19.35	13.65
175	26.60	22.58	15.93
200	30.40	25.80	18.20
225	34.20	29.03	20.48
240	36.48	30.96	21.84
260	39.52	33.54	23.66
280	42.56	36.12	25.48
300	45.60	38.70	27.30
350	53.20	45.15	31.85
400	60.80	51.60	36.40
450	68.40	58.05	40.95
500	76.00	64.50	45.50
750	114.00	96.75	68.25
1,000	152.00	129.00	91.00

Rates correct at time of going to press November 2000

Spoofs

All our books have the odd spoof hidden away within their pages. Sunken boats, telephone boxes and ruined castles have all featured. Some of you have written in with your own ideas, so we have decided to hold a competition for spoof writing every year.

The rules are simple: send us your own spoofs, include the photos, and let us know which book it is intended for. We will publish the winning entries in the following edition of each book. We will also send you a complete set of our guides to each winner.

Please send your entries to:

Alastair Sawday Publishing, Spoofs competition, The Home Farm, Barrow Gurney, Bristol BS48 3RW. Winners will be notified by post.

Symbols

Symbols

Treat each one as a guide rather than a statement of fact and check important points when booking:

 Disabled facilities provided.

 Pets are welcome as long as they are properly trained and docile. There may be a supplement to pay or size restrictions.

 Modem connections available.

 Lift installed. It may stop short of the top floor or start on the first floor.

 Restaurant. The hotel has its own restaurant or a separately-managed restaurant next door.

 Air conditioning in bedrooms. It may be a centrally-operated system or individual apparatus.

 Payment by cash only.

LA FIN

John Pruen
20 July 1914 - 24 October 1999